EMOTIONAL
ENGINEERING

EMOTIONAL ENGINEERING

CURE AND MENTAL EMPOWERMENT THROUGH
INTRAPERSONAL COMMUNICATION BASED
ON HANDWRITING ANALYSIS WITH GRAPHOTHERAPIES

Dr Raghvendra Kumar

PARTRIDGE

To order additional copies of this book, contact
Partridge India
000 800 10062 62
orders.india@partridgepublishing.com

www.partridgepublishing.com/india

CONTENTS

ABOUT THE BOOK

This book is completely original and based on my own entrepreneur research, in which most of psychiatric issues with full of explanations and therapy are considered. Along with curing illnesses applying adequate intrapersonal communication according to the unique personality based on Emotional Mechanism through handwriting analysis, this book is very helpful for deep and better understanding cure of mental disorders as most of the disorders are profoundly discussed in this book.

Method used in curing illnesses discussed in this is book passed under strict and critic supervision of psychiatrist and cases referred to me were most of chronic and supposed incurable for psychiatry. At the same time, all patients had supposed that they are compelled to consume psychiatric medicines throughout life. "Emotional Engineering" as "curing and mental empowerment too" is proven 100% successful. During testing, I was referred 21 chronic cases and all became cured and were freed from psychiatric medication within period of 4 to 8 weeks. Surprisingly the "Emotional Engineering" is not only cure with proper mental empowerment but also very fast as quick healing without medication. On this basis, this method of curing with mental empowerment is termed as "Emotional Medication".

I was fully focused on curing psychiatric issues with mental empowerment using intrapersonal communication based on understanding emotional mechanism that is handwriting analysis but during testing a case came to of hypertension-ridden person who was regular consuming medicines. That was my first case of non-psychiatry; I applied "Emotional Engineering" in which I given "therapeutic personality research report" with set of "graphotherapies" to insist person for required intrapersonal communication according to personality and surprisingly on following my instructions, patient became completely ok just within 4 weeks and need of medicines was then no more to him. Then I thought this is actually most advance tool to cure all problems related to mind either directly or indirectly. Later on, I applied this tool on many endocrine disorders and other problems caused by stress. Understanding "Emotional Mechanism" of person, I applied "Emotional Engineering" to bring exact reform in particular fundamental personality traits via brain learning towards setting "neural pathways" of personality traits, there were more than enough reform occurred in patients and gradually they became completely ok.

Hither in recent days, many motivational teachers came out in market without studying emotional system of personality and they deliver even common data to all in their motivational seminar, class or gatherings. Theoretically, speech what they deliver to people is suitable for just one person whereas, for rest of people that is rather harmful for personal emotional system of person. The given data (preach) to attending people is just either more than requirement of personality or lesser because there were no study of personality of each person who are attending seminar or class. On getting more than required data mind becomes confused while on lesser data mind refuses rudely all throughout. In fact, all speech to be delivered to the people is just mind ethnic without serious study in any form or at any level. Actually, they are farcing with the people in the name of motivation. There are so many cases come out of depression, OCD, phobia and personality disorders just because of either reading motivational books or attending motivational classes of motivational teachers. No major change either in personality still reported except for the loss by means of that so-called motivations in corporate or in general. After all, without personal study, it quite impossible to make adequate personal data towards any type of motivation. Despite their personal active appearances, there is no positive change in society. Corruption, immoral conduct and many other social misdeeds are still growing up. They are just charlatan in field of mind. Public and corporate must avoid such motivational charlatans because they are in the way of deteriorating natural emotional system of person even despite they are paid.

Many people are often seen crazy about knowing their future. This is very dangerous thing. First thing is that no one can tell about future except like it will rain in rainy season means all foretellers sheer lie in this concern. The sheer lie also deteriorates natural emotional system of person by making them bias which leads person to focus himself on that topic which is likely to be impossible and in this effort person tries to ignore essential conditional factors which would be very necessary in developmental thrive of person. Second thing is if by chance you are told about your exact future it will also be dangerous because person drastically focuses on results to get as soon as possible as he was told about. This precocity normally get person in anxiety may lead to Phobia, OCD, Panic Disorder etc. Therefore, craze of knowing future is very dangerous to every person and therefore people must avoid it.

As far as hormonal disorders are concerned, this book is quite much helpful for such people who are thinking that without medicines they cannot go even one-step in their life. Such thinking in fact is due to hormonal disorder. As "Emotional Engineering" directly works on emotional system through neural pathways of personality traits and endocrine equilibrium directly depends upon the emotional system of the person. Therefore, applying "Emotional Engineering" is the actual effort towards correcting hormonal imbalance without medication within few weeks and becoming free from medicinal dependency and side effects as well.

CHAPTER – 1

Preface

"Emotional Engineering is "Understanding Emotional Mechanism to bring change in personality with required manipulation in unique emotional system of person through intrapersonal communication by therapeutic graphological personality research report with graphotherapies towards mental empowerment leads cure."

Without mental empowerment, cure is not possible which is seriously missing in this age. "Emotional engineering" that is intrapersonal communication based Grapho-psychiatry is far advance than current running technique because of having quick healing and cures within few weeks with proper mental empowerment. According to one the most prominent graphologist of the world, President of Handwriting University International, USA, Bart Andrew Baggette "it takes person just 28 days in ideal condition" that is far too fast rather than any medication. It is commonly seen that many patients of mood disorders, anxiety disorders, personality disorders, hypertension, hormonal disorders, schizophrenia etc. are compel to take medication for decades or even throughout life. What does it mean? It is clear fact that system of medication has no cure. Many accidents or mishaps of suicide and massacre are reported despite even being under medication with counseling along. This fact is also endorsed by a human right activist organization in many countries including USA.

Actually all medication is run on very guess only that is why the possibility of curing becomes too feeble because of tolerance of brain and being highly sensitive emotional system of mind works in different way, remain always untouched by the medication at best. As researches on artificial intelligence are becoming, the fact comes out that our mind absolutely works on neural pathway system of personality traits, which is responsible for making of our unique emotional system that actually makes biochemistry of body and brain as well. Therefore, problems do not occur due to chemical imbalance as it is claimed. Problems actually occur in personality traits owing to external factors and due to which malfunctioning take place through misperception, misunderstanding and so on, which lead distortion in "neural pathways of personality traits".

Yet in any system, there was no method to diagnose exact state of mind in grater context of personality and their trait. Therefore, on any level psychological problems are still incurable by that current running system. There are so many cases of acute depression, who manages to commit suicide instead of being under medication. In fact, those patients are under medication without diagnosis of their personality status regarding exact form of traits. Like depression, there are so many other patients of other mental disorder-ridden are under lifelong medication but instead of being benefitted, they become addicted of. Without proper diagnosis towards knowing emotional mechanism, no disorder can be cured by any mean.

It is well known fact about brain that brain consists of dense network of neurons and each neuron is filled with exact data to regulate body and other functions. All these data come from intrapersonal communication. These exact data came from circumstances and conditional factors through intrapersonal communication are specific form different personality traits and cluster of traits form personality of person that forms unique "mind". The specific data are provided to neurons by learning which starts since sixth month of mother's womb, yes off course it also takes place just through intrapersonal communication varies person to person and according to condition make personality unique through intrapersonal communication. The specific neurons with specific data are called "neural pathways" of traits. The forms of traits are directly responsible for functioning body and other mode of thinking as well. Since all function and thinking method are unique so, handwriting pattern of person is unique. This reflects exact form of traits and whole personality. Thus, handwriting is in fact "Writing of Mind" or "Mind Manuscript" that can be said. This way handwriting reveals exact form of traits and personality.

As on looking into handwriting, we come to know exact form of traits and personality and in same way, we can bring change in personality through bringing change in handwriting termed as "graphotherapy" is very helpful to make scope of desired intrapersonal communication. Moreover, the role of "graphotherapy" is to create new neural pathways to feed exact data according to demand of unique personality towards mental empowerment that is the actual cure of illnesses. After formation of new neural pathways, it necessary to feed exact data come from understanding "emotional mechanism" of person's unique personality handwriting undergoes to micro level analysis on "trait by trait" method towards desired intrapersonal communication. The analysis of handwriting makes available the exact data to be communicated in new pathways via brain learning through intrapersonal communication. The analysis report is then converted into "therapeutic personality research report" by adding required "guidance suggestions" based on "all or none" theory on active "fundamental personality traits". This is the perfect way of intrapersonal communication towards brain learning. These suggestions are just according to the demand of person's unique personality. The data to be communicated to the mind must be in adequate amount otherwise if that will more than requirement mind will get confused while on lesser data mind will rudely refuse them. Both conditions are dangerous for the individual. Communication must be adequate and according to the unique personality. Mind accepts only adequate data on its own unique emotional ground. This way using intrapersonal communication, we manipulate particular trait for particular purpose. Therefore, "therapeutic personality research report" with "graphotherapies" is perfect "Emotional Engineering" through which we empower mind up to infinite level. It is found that on communicating exact data, mind accepts all those instantly and go for learning because neural pathways are very communicating in nature. Neural pathways of traits are always in prompt towards communication by nature.

There are four basics or fundamentals of "human emotional system" and support of human personality –

1. Pleasure
2. Danger
3. Ego and
4. Sex

Complete human psychology depends upon these 4 fundamentals, these may also be called as "Four fundamental Pillars of Emotional System" and all these must be in balanced form according to unique personality. Whenever due to any external factor any disturbance comes across these 4 fundamentals through distortion in neural pathways of personality traits, not only mental disorders take place but also biochemistry body get disturbed that may lead to physical disorders. Therefore, it is very necessary to keep all these in natural and balanced form according to the personality. The healthy personality needs adequate balanced sensitivity and sensibility along.

There are "three basic causes" behind all mental disorders, which are just basic requirement and purpose of personality. These are –

1. Security
2. Communication and
3. Sociality

All four fundamental pillars and basic requirements of emotional system are interdependent upon each other and work vice-versa. It can be observed easily that pleasure needs all three basics in positive, danger needs all three but in negative, ego needs all three in peak either in positive or negative and sex also needs all three basic parts of emotional system security, sociality and communication are not only in positive form but in creative form also. On any sort of disturbance in basic requirement of emotional system, mental disorder takes place. These three fundamentals are directly governed by neural pathway system of personality traits.

According to basic fundamental of "genetics" no DNA pattern of any two individuals even if why not they are just twins, can be exactly same, on same pattern no all protein structure of any two individuals can be same which result nature of any two individuals cannot be exactly same. Likewise this, the emotional system of any two individuals cannot be same which basic and fundamental reason is of difference in handwritings of any two individuals even if twins. It is found in study that handwriting of all children in initial stages is about it and gradually as their personality develops, differences come out according to their mentality. The mental development of any two individuals is not same therefore their handwriting also cannot be exactly same.

As unique emotional system of a person accomplishes his unique handwriting pattern likewise that through unique handwriting the unique psycho system, form of traits and scope of function of person can be identified easily. This is in fact the way of identifying state of mind regarding traits which govern behavior (normal and abnormal both) of person and there after it becomes so easy to create vast possibilities for person with curing illnesses through mental empowerment along.

"Emotional Engineering" affects vast area in which every field of person's working comes. No field of working and thinking is exception of this advance tool. This advance tool is far useful all types of people either they are normal behavior showing normal people or the most complex and intricate behavior showing people (philosophers). Including stress, complexes, ego conflict all type of mental disorders and mentality born physical disorders are curable quick and permanently. It is often found that there are so many cases of acute depression attempted for suicide even being under psychiatric medication and psychological treatment. Such types of cases can be fully checked with the help of this advance tool of intrapersonal communication with complete mental empowerment. As mentality born physical disorders like diabetes, hypertension, hormonal disorders and other after treatment by which person becomes so irritating concern, "Emotional Engineering" is very useful in managing their stress and causes of irritation and because of those many of these cause of death in many cases. Through mental empowerment by "Emotional Engineering", people reasonably be kept free many problems and through this healing process may increase in leaps and bounds as well if he comes in needs of. Because all physiology including brain are strictly governed by mind.

Regarding mental disorders there is fact that reasons behind those are conditions and responses of mind. That is why all mental disorders have external stimulus as cause. Curing such behavioral abnormality becomes very easy through "Emotional Engineering" without medication.

"Emotional Engineering" holds concept of mental empowerment significantly rather than others. For better survival, person must be efficient to work worthy than being disorder less inefficient. That clear means it has strong capability of opening possibilities of development and thrive for people and all things are just depend upon only handwriting. It is quite natural and according to his unique personality. Therefore, there is nothing unnatural in the advance therapy that is why it is so pleasant, natural, interesting and impeccable.

There are even many factors behind success of this therapy; the most significant reason among them is "capability of exact diagnosing state of mind on micro level of personality traits" with problems unbiased. It is quite impossible to get complete data from client using schedule, question or interview. It is found that no question could be unbiased, it is seen many times client has problem in understanding, perception and in saying. At the same time, there is another problem whether expert can access to the exact cause of problem or not. This therapy is quite free from all these obstructions. Our nervous system and mind work on "All or None" theory, so it is very necessary towards learning mind through intrapersonal communication, data given to client must be in 'exact and complete' form and according to the personality. Otherwise, our mind will rudely 'refuse' that if data is less than complete and on other hand if given data is more than need then our mind will get 'confuse'. Both stages rejection and confusion are very dangerous for clients. 'Emotional Engineering' is quite free from such problem which makes it to the point therapy with full of success because it provides complete data according to the unique personality so mind does not get reactive and accept all data towards Mental Empowerment.

According to many modern researches on physiology of brain that it works on neural pathway system of traits. The fact about Mental Empowerment is that this is only possible when Emotional Engineering creates new neural pathways of traits in brain through learning via intrapersonal communication, which is only possible in easy way. In fact, brain is filled with dense network of neurons and our traits are pathway of neurons in specific pattern, which differ person to person according to unique nature. These pathways get started formed in womb since six or seventh month and since that time personality of person becomes started taking shape. Formation and deformation go on throughout life this natural phenomenon. This is very theory on which artificial intelligence of robots are being developed. For the time being because of directly working on neural pathway system of personality traits nothing is better than Emotional Engineering for mental empowerment.

As far as mental disorders is concerned there is fact regarding that is due to any or many "external stimulus" distortion takes place in neural pathways of traits and due to which the "cognitive system" of mind becomes disturbed and mind starts giving abnormal reactions on specific action or without even being no action too. There is very simple logic in this concern is if pathways of personality traits are reformed and get them correlated with other supporting personality traits then mental and related physical illnesses are cured within few weeks with proper mental empowerment. Emotional Engineering is not less than a boon for those who are bothered by mental disorder, abnormal behavior, low intelligence and any mental born physical problems.

CHAPTER – 2

Scope of Emotional Engineering

In Vedic era of ancient India, there were so many people of super human types. It means men with supernatural power or fantastic talents. Such people are generally different from others because of having such supernatural power or fantastic talents, known as Rishi, Maharshi, Bramharshi, Sadhoo, Saint etc. According to a context of "Mahabharata" the son of Guru Dronacharya, Ashwatthama had power of 2000 elephants. Yes, of course he had. On psychological ground there are two types of in our brain one is conscious mind and second subconscious mind. Subconscious mind is about 2000 times bigger than conscious mind and beyond voluntary control. We cannot use consciously subconscious mind normally. However, we can by deep and devoted and efforts called "Sadhana or Tapasya" to control subconscious mind and use that consciously. Every might will be 2000 times, of what person has as power. In ancient time Bramharshi, Maharshi etc used to go to jungle, mountains or any no men's land for Sadhana-Tapasya (penance) for specific learning and then use that by conscious mind in general practice. Ashwatthama had ability to use subconscious mind consciously like many other chivalry.

"Emotional Engineering" is based on the concept to insist person towards empowering his subconscious mind by proper and specific intrapersonal communication and use that in particular contexts as per requirement. However, Sadhana-Tapasya (Penence) is far bigger subject but this is an effort towards this direction. Being mentally healthy is not sufficient but we have to be quite powerful on mental and physical level both. "Power always dwells in mind than physique".

Emotional Engineering ensures perfect way of "Emotional Management" according to unique personality of an individual that what type of emotions are to used in general or specifically and how much in greater context of time which is fixed for everyone in macro and micro level as well. For example, a person may be in huge lose socially, financially and even security concerns if he does not use his emotions adequately but he would be definitely in benefits if uses his emotions intelligently. The significance of emotional management has the greatest importance in life because every occasion may be consist of opportunities that can change even in a moment.

Especially this book is mostly centralized on psychiatric and mind related issues but "Emotional Engineering" is rather useful for not only problem facing person but also for them who are normal, holding concept "all functions and processes of our body depend upon thinking and emotional mechanism". It clearly means that form of intrapersonal communication is the root cause of mental activities either positive or negative. On applying "Emotional Engineering", the normal people can also improve their own "mental efficiency" through mental empowerment. This is very useful for individuals who are intellectual. With the help of "Emotional Engineering", all types of mental and mentality born physical disorders can be kept away forever on applying this advance tool as preventive measure and through which huge amount of monetary and health resources can be save avoiding side effects of medicines. In fact, side effects of medication are new sites from where new diseases are generated which is very big problem in itself.

Only "all or none" theory is effective in bringing change in personality traits. Without knowing facts on micro-level diagnosis about unique personality, it is quite impossible to bring any sort of change in person. In curing through mental empowerment, it may be quite harmful using single staff for all cattle. Here all cattle need its own staff according to their own unique personality to bring changes in them. A single pattern of curing is not applicable for all people.

Emotional Engineering covers almost every area related to the mind and cognitive approaches as well. Every system of our body and mind as well, are under strict control of mind through its emotional system. Here I will discuss the fields in which Emotional Engineering works successfully in addition to psychiatric disorders. The main and basic feature of its working is "Mental Empowerment" through which it becomes very powerful tool to transform personality as per demand. Because of direct working it on "neural pathway system", the process of Mental Empowerment becomes very fast takes just 28 days in ideal conditions. In general conditions, it may take hardly 1 to 2 months approx. There are following fields –

1. Enhancing Immune System, Correcting Endocrine Disorders and other Physical Problems

Our immune system completely depends upon emotional system. If emotional system is not in right or pleasant way to then surely the immune system will not be correct. On holding this concept, if emotional system is corrected then it is sure that immune system will also be enhanced. How it could be much? Yes, it would be 100% as much it should be. "Emotional Engineering" is so advance science through which immune system can be enhanced up to 100% through mental empowerment using "Emotional Engineering".

(A) In Correction of Eosinophil Count

About 2 years ago, a case came to me of 24-year-old man was under psychiatric treatment of depression diagnosed had been suffering since last 11 years. On not getting any benefit, he changed 3-4 psychiatrists but rather than getting benefitted the case was on gradual deterioration. He told me there was stomach problem to him about 12 year back and on even prolonged treatment he did not cure then someone told him to consult psychiatrist because in some psychiatric problems gastric problem is a common phenomenon then he must go for treatment of depression rather than of gastric problem. He took psychiatric treatment but lastly he came to me. At that time case had become so complicated and his eyes were so heavy to open normal, he was in so drowsiness and was also too slack in somewhat sleepy. On Emotional mechanism research of his handwriting, I found he is not only depression ridden but also suffering from severe anxiety disorder (OCD). In diagnosis, I found depression based on OCD. I prepared therapeutic personality research report to make his mind learn to create, reform or both neural pathways of personality traits through intrapersonal communication. On taking him about 2 months, he became completely rid of psychiatric problems. Moreover, just after that on phone he told me that his eosinophilia has also been cured, I was surprised at that time and asked him how did he come to know that he was also patient of eosinophilia? He replied me that he has been under regular blood examination for last 10 years. According to blood-report the level of eosinophils was around 20% by count for last 11 years, which was quite more than normal (4-6%) and lymphocyte was 21-24 %. On my behalf, I made his blood examination then found the lymphocyte has become 46% by count. This was 100% (just double) enhancement. Now patient has completely rid of problem of eosinophilia. "Emotional Engineering" did this without medication. Well, in allopathy there is no cure of such immune problem except consuming immune suppressive drugs while attack, which is quite unhealthy and dangerous with serious side effects. "Emotional Engineering" made patient so empowered that immunity became 100% strong and even incurable illness such as eosnophilia cured. Now a day patient is taking all dishes like rice, onion, radish, curd etc. easily like other health people, which were creating problem and that is why prohibited to him.

(B)   In curing Insomnia

With the help of "Emotional Engineering", insomnia like serious illness is curable in easy and pleasant way without medication within few weeks. Indeed the reasons behind this illness are only mental which may originate either from anxiety or high level stress. Either misuse of traits or any external stimulus may cause such anxiety, mood problems or stress etc. leads to insomnia because of unwanted distortion occurred in neural pathways of personality traits. Sleeping pills are not treatment of insomnia because it generates illusion of sleep instead of bringing natural sleep and gradually patient get into habit of these pills. On waking up in the morning after sleep with sleeping pills, person do not feel fresh like natural sleep. He feels even tired, irritating and aggressiveness rather than relaxed. Because of such these problems person feels much difficulties in establishing reconciliation among his daily routine behavior and among other factors. Since, reason is mental and due to distortion in neural pathways of personality traits, therefore it is so easy to cure it using "Emotional Engineering" through mental empowerment. After cure mind of person becomes far empowered than before and person is freed to take sleeping pills.

About 7 years ago, a case of 29-year-old person came to me. However, he was not good in reading but was very good athlete in DDU Gorakhpur University. Because of this, his expectations were so high which could not be met out. The dissent caused him high stress and insomnia took him in grip. He also took medication for 2 years but result was cipher. He came to me cured by "Emotional Engineering". He was not only cured within few weeks but also his mind became so empowered to take more interest in reading and started study from new end. He cleared B.Ed. with good marks and after he is now a teacher and spending honored healthy life with full of natural sleep. With the help of "Emotional Engineering", his mind became quite powerful and more than normal.

(C)   In Curing Hypertension and Endocrine Imbalances

"Emotional Engineering" is very much useful in curing problem of hypertension and most of the endocrine problem. Through this so advance tool, on reforming or developing new neural pathways of personality traits, the physical health can improve via brain learning towards specific and holistic mental empowerment as well via adequate intrapersonal communication. As far as hypertension is concerned, according to WHO data India about 140 million people is suffering from this dangerous problem leads to renal failure, paralysis and on psycho ground disturbance in behavior that results poor relationships. Physician advices patients to take medicine throughout life that results patients get into the habit of that medicine and as time passes tolerance against those medicines and dose of medicine increases as increasing tolerance that means as medicine is consumed disease increases accordingly. In side-by-side patient have to face side effects of drugs additionally. The "Emotional Engineering" provides quick and permanent cure without medication with mental empowerment.

A case 24-year-old male patient had been suffering from hypertension since 3 years and was compel to take medicine regularly. With the help of "Emotional Engineering", he became complete rid off this problem within few weeks and compulsion of consuming medicine was no more to him.

As far as problems of endocrine are concerned completely depends upon emotional system of individual. On occurring correction in emotional system with intrapersonal communication towards mental empowerment, problems are easily curable without medication. A case of very learned person of my city came to me about 9 years ago with complaint of unable to feel differences among days of weeks. Because of that, he could not set his routine accordingly. I prepared his therapeutic graphological research report for intrapersonal communication towards brain learning for mental empowerment and handover him after full demonstration. Nevertheless, he had to go SGPGI, Lucknow to consult regarding same problem. After complete examination, he was diagnosed adrenaline disorder and he was advised to correct his life style and bring somewhat in thinking but no medicine he was prescribed. The advises were in few points where as therapeutic Emotional Mechanism personality research report was complete personality report then he convinced with this advance therapy and on following that report he had become complete healthy within 1 month with proper mental empowerment. Likewise this many other endocrine problem can be cured with this advance "Emotional Engineering".

2. Mental Empowerment in Corporate, Care and Cure

In fact, Emotional Engineering is far useful for all who works under high level of stress, anxiety, mood disturbing etc like environment. It is commonly observed that all personals who work under serious workload are supposed to be get mood, anxiety and personality disorder-ridden leads to suppressed intelligence and ultimately work efficiency becomes badly affected, which results decrement in profit of particular corporate. At the same time, the work environment also becomes affected negatively leads to reduction of corporate business. This advance Emotional Engineering tool is not only a perfect solution of all such problems but also it has quite better scope in recruitments to select appropriate and suitable candidates, HR department to utilize maximum potential of employees with humanistic cardiac care, emerging employees with full of occupationally devoted and employees could be reassigned according to their potential. Therefore, the HR department of corporate should have "potential profile" of employees to assign or reassign. The "potential profile" of employee must be clear data based using "advance analysis tool" as understanding "Emotional Mechanism" of them.

In corporate world, high management officials who works on edge of high level stress, depression, Anxiety, insomnia, hypertension, and so on and all these problems direct affects business in negative way, can not only get rid completely off such problems but also they will get quite mentally empowered to convert problems into opportunities just within few weeks.

For example, a serious and chronic case of a depression was referred to me. The case was of CA and he had been under psychiatric medication since 12 years. He got completely rid this problem off by Emotional Engineering within just 2 months and with full of Mental empowerment along. There is no need of dangerous drugs to him now and he is developing quite fast in his business using all opportunities, which were problems for him before mental empowerment. In addition to this, there are so many normal management officials got promotion after mental empowerment by "Emotional Engineering".

CURRENT MENTAL PROBLEMS – According to the studies there are about one-fifth population of United States of America is suffering from "depression" above adolescent. Surprisingly numbers of female under depression are more than male because of emotional factors. It is dangerous situation towards making strong emotional bondage among members of family. Most of them are not able to work properly which is huge lose of society, corporate, country and resources as well. Jobs are not now easy to meet out the assignment and most of them are seriously looking for other options to do jobs and avoiding direct their involvement. This is double hammer wound of just depression. Therefore, mental problem is very serious issue to resolve immediately.

EMPLOYEE'S MENTAL PROBLEMS - "Emotional Engineering" is quite helpful in meeting all problems out which are barrier in development. There are clear facts about corporate that -

a. Corporate are not able to exploit complete potential and talent of employees.
b. Due to being of workload as external stimulus and others, employees fall in to severe stress that results subsidence in work efficiency that causes many mental disorders.
c. Some employees feel difficulties in their usual circumstances and they have to do much more efforts even towards maintain their normal performance. They are failing in using themselves in positive way.
d. In technology and BPO sector, the problems become more serious where reasonability and intelligence have to be used quite more than other sectors. In fact, mental problems take place when logic power is abnormally more used than that of employee's efficiency creates much pressure regarding this concern. Mental and mental born physical problems are being often observed in plenty and because of false personality presentation personality disorders and hormonal disorders due to odd timing of work in all BPO sectors.
e. Well, to vanquish these problems, the corporate are doing serious efforts but those are quite inadequate, insufficient and many where fail.

Mental disorders and problems are stigmatized in many countries cultures and organizations too (Weis and others 2001). Slow emergence of exact convincing scientific explanation for the etiologies of mental disorders and false belief that symptoms caused by lack of will power or show moral taints. Combined with educational efforts, recent scientific findings have started to reduce that stigma (Rahman and other 1998). The result of are disparities, compare with other illnesses, inviolability of care & cure, in research and in abuses of the human rights of human being with other disorders. But fear and shame still attached with mental disorders remain obstructions to seek and probe, to diagnosis perfectly and to cure.

The following objectives can be accomplished by applying "Emotional Engineering" in corporate -

(i)   Corporate mental empowerment, care and cure
(ii)   Drastic improvement of mental and working potential by mental advancement
(iii) Keep corporate away from negative vibrations
(iv)   Complete employee motivation towards corporate monetary development.
(v)   Conflict correction in occupational values
(vi)   To utilize mental resources for its maximum performance
(vii) To modify traits as desired
(viii) To spot red and danger signals in any one personality
(ix)   To develop optimistic views in employees to accept challenges that may significant cause of enhancing benefits of corporate in multiply.
(x)   The "Emotional Engineering" significantly will help in selection of employee weather psychologically deserving or not. By this way, the corporate will be away from bitter taste of recession in future.

3.   Development of Leadership Quality

"Emotional Engineering' is far advance to develop any talent from its initial point. Since every person has his unique personality so on only going on micro-level diagnosis any development of talent can be insured according to unique personality and the mode of learning that varies personality to personality. Therefore, every person has different emotional system so development must be according to the personality otherwise mind will be reactive or confused which may result new course mental problems. One method of brain learning is not applicable on other one as such. Without deep and micro-level diagnosis of personality, it is not possible, this is dead sure. Since only handwriting analysis has ability of micro-level diagnosis of personality so, only "Emotional Engineering" can do it in easy way within couple of months. Well generally, it is very necessary of being 13 traits in personality of a good, honest and strenuous leader in any field either of politics, social work, organizational, or corporate. For example being knowledge of history of concerned matter, clear point of view, studiousness, self-confidence, strong reasonability, and strong sociality, prospective nature, power of imagination to make vision, ability of planning, responsibility feeling, optimism, patience, communicating nature and ability of listening others with patience. In addition to these being of other strong traits, give different recognition to the leader. If any leader posses at least these 13 traits, it will be quite impossible to defeat him on any level. Towards developing leadership quality, all these 13 traits will be then necessary to develop and all personality will have to be empowered as well at a time otherwise overall leadership quality in a person will not be developed at all. Therefore, it is possible to do on the clear base of personality.

Well, one who already in the field of leadership is and problem ridden with his job then through intrapersonal communication driven "Emotional Engineering" can be rooted out providing proper mental empowerment towards effective leadership that is beyond imagination of traditional psychology and psychiatry.

4. Development of Talents

In comparison to traditional psychology the Emotional Engineering is rather advance through which it is possible to empower or can get human mind reach to any extant very quickly. Unlike traditional psychology, Emotional Engineering every person of every class of society like businessman, medical professionals, engineering professional, management professionals, students from KG to Ph.D. and professional courses, housewives etc. can be benefited with this advance form of science. To get its benefits it is not necessary to be a psychopath, all healthy person can get Mentally Empowered with the help of this. Using this advance therapy of Mental Empowerment, anyone can get new heights of success in their life, which is based on person's own personality instead of being based on others. Therefore, there is no possibility of abnormal stress, anxiety and pressure in this therapy. Unlike other psychological therapies, this advance therapy is even highly pleasant.

Since all this without medication so there is no possibility of side effect. The rate of its success is 100% provided client follows all given instructions.

All talents are specific and goal focused having its many targets, defined as in a specific context, on adjusting all essential personality traits to meet contemporary target out towards goal determined within time allotted. Here time is very important factor if specific time is not in target or goal is not a talent. Each talent of every field has its unique property having specific set of essential personality traits. In natural way in talented person, required traits work compositely for achieving specific goal or target where as in normal or talent lacking person traits do not work together towards specific goal. With the help of Emotional Engineering all essential traits identified accordingly, as they are in unique personality and all traits will be set according specific talent.

For example if a person wants to be a writer then firstly it will be necessary to see inside of his personality to indentify the exact form of his active traits being used by him that will determine area of writing and then with the full potential of all essential personality traits will be set according to the talent. The process generally takes person 2 to 3 months and on gradual practicing, person gets honed talent. This is the only way through which any type of talent like being cricketer, shuttler and other sport skill, artist, scientist, writer, painter, actor, lawyer, businessperson etc. can be developed in any person in format of his own personality having unique identification. Being differences in talents, it is very necessary for further development.

Simultaneously the lost form of talented persons can be retrieved and provided them back in more strong with more intelligence form than before by this advance science. In cases of lost form, the fact behind this phenomenon is mind of talented person get into in "resting phase" which beyond control of person or any other psychological method or tool. In "resting phase" the particular intelligence regarding talent becomes ineffective and then no logic no confidence, no skill work towards specific target or goal. Therefore, only way remains to the person that is wait and watch. However, with the help of Emotional Engineering person can retrieve lost form in quite more empowered format than before. "Talent retrieving mechanism" is applicable in all fields like development of sport, artistry, advocacy, science and so on.

5. Solution of Problems of Different Level Students and Fields

Students of different level face have many problems related to their behavior, personality and overall intelligence because of being many external and internal factors. All these factors direct affect performance of students. The "Emotional Engineering" provides perfect solution with mental empowerment.

A. Problems of Adolescents (10th and 10+2 Students)

Most of students of this age group are highly concerned with coming new life and career. This is because of adolescent over zeal, abnormal seriousness, sexual feelings with changes in body, bio-chemical changes etc are factors to give shape to the personality. If these are not in appropriate form and direction may cause serious problems like illusion and blurredness towards goal of life. All around and everywhere, the coeducation system of schooling made problem more serious. Increasing number of suicide cases due to mood disorders, anxiety disorders, personality disorders and so on. As students must focus themselves on their career coeducation gives extra burden of competition, fight and route diversion of thinking which may form chain of mental disorders on different levels. "Emotional Engineering" provides perfect and permanent solution of such problems with proper mental empowerment.

B. Problems of General Students

General Students of non professional academic fields of B.A., M.A., B.Sc., M.Sc., B.Com., M.Com. and like other courses are mostly often worried about their future and in confusion as well. Since they are not in profession courses, so they are found him quite insecure and have severe problem in goal setting that leads to dependency on other's opinions, and compel to accept any proposal with halfhearted mind they fail to deliver their best performance to the institution. That would result neither institution able to develop properly nor person. "Emotional Engineering" is the very best medium to self-explore towards better career and deliverance of best performance as well with mental empowerment.

C. Problems of Professional Students

It is often seen that most of students comes in high stress as they take admission in professional courses and become complex stricken as well. Well, being no option to them situation becomes serious. This is the very reason that students of IIT, AIIMS and alike others, get into the habit of addiction. Drinking has become so common that no one takes it otherwise these days. Surprisingly, female students are also coming in same problem from exception drastically. Depression, anxiety, personality disorders are common nowadays lead to increment in suicide cases, poor performance and dissidence in their lives causing many other serious problems. Only "Emotional Engineering" can save such professional students from such mental disaster through proper mental empowerment.

There are so many cases of professional students including suicide attempted have been cured this advance science with proper mental empowerment.

D. Problems of Research Scholars

All research scholars must have "high mental ability" which is needed too much towards high-level research. This is only possible when scholar will use his mind in innovative way. On doing this in one hand, he could complete his research on or before with converting problems into opportunities time and in other hand if there is any possibility of any invention or discovery researcher can sense easily during research. To do all such things mind needs quite different type of "analytical ability" which can be provided by "Emotional Engineering" because of being concept of mental empowerment is only here.

Well, all researches are work of full stress and high mental pressure that creates high possibilities of many mental disorders like depression, anxiety disorders, personality disorders and many other problems to which scholar may be stricken. Because of these problems, the mental ability of scholar gets direct affected which big & major loss leads deteriorations in quality of researches in side-by-side. The "Emotional Engineering" make scholar free all problems and keep doing such enhances mental ability through mental empowerment. Through this advance tool, history can be created.

A research scholar in physics was psychic problem-stricken and had been under psychiatric medication for 6 months. He became complete cured with the help of "Emotional Engineering" with full of mental empowerment.

E.   Problems of Students Preparing For Competitive Exams

Students who are preparing for beating competitive exams with the help of coaching or who are doing without, all face and suffer with high mental pressure, stress due to high competitive feelings and high level of anxiety causing fear. To face all such problems and preparation for exam as in expected level. With the help of "Emotional Engineering", it is possible to enhance mental ability keeping them away from such problems with empowering mind. This advance tool ensures betterment in intelligent memory, imaginary power, reasonability, opportunity management, stress management, ability of taking quick decision rational exchange and other vital personality traits.

There were so many cases came to me from Kota, Lucknow and Kanpur of coaching students of different subject and fields were in acute depression with feeling of suicide, OCD and with gastric problem due to high level of stress and psycho problems. Though all big coaching institutes have psychologist despite its problem is serious because traditional psychology and psychiatry has no solution. All students were become cured with the help of "Emotional Engineering" with proper mental empowerment and ultimately they succeeded in getting selection.

However, it is believed and even true that passing competitive exams are just "trick" rather than actual evaluation of knowledge and their application that results many incompetent candidates get succeeded in beating competitions. Such candidates are also major problem in form of burden for society and system as they lack many important and significant traits in their personality. Therefore, the "Emotional Engineering" is also a perfect solution for such serious problem.

6. Problems in Judiciary Services

People engaged in judiciary services have to face many types of problems like high pressure, high level of stress due to searching favorable evidences and anxiety of winning case. They have to do pleasant and reasonable communication with clients and related persons in every condition. While in court, they have to face another type of stress of keeping their side reasonable to be winner all time. If person fail to manage all such problems then it is likely to be supposed that they may be problem-stricken mentally. Same things are also applicable on judges also but having differences of communication with clients as they are free from this. With the help of 'Emotional Engineering" they get freedom from such problems and get succeeded in to reconcile among traits and become mentally empowered.

A case came to me about 2 years ago of session court judge had been under psychiatric medication for since 3 years because of being diagnosed OCD. There was no benefit to him by psychiatry. "Emotional Engineering" made him complete rid off OCD and dangerous medicines as well within 3 weeks with full of mental empowerment.

7. In Journalism

Journalism is field where journalists have to cover always new events as no happening repeats itself any time and all news must have to present in its own psychology being covered events keeping all norms, restrictions and social customs in mind. At the same time, journalist towards sensing news journalists need to have high level of sensibility, sensitivity, reasonability and high ability of analyzing data received etc. If all related traits are in balanced and strong form then journalist will be able to give new heights through journalism by agenda setting, social education and sound messaging.

The "Emotional Engineering" is very strong and helpful tool in emerging effective and strong journalism towards strengthen the fourth pillar of democracy. Recently its is being observed that most of journalist are quite fail to read "public attitude" that results declination in credibility which must be procured. All journalist strictly must have the ability of understanding "public mood, public perception and public opinion" on various matter. Such these disabilities lead society in "social illusion" which is creating social disappointment on mass scale. Therefore, it is very necessary for all journalists strictly have ability of understanding "public attitude".

Well in general, many journalists face mental problems due to workload, misinterpretation analysis, mistiming of working and other social anxiety creating problems facing in work field, they come or supposed to come into grip of mental disorders. "Emotional Engineering" is perfect solution in rid them off permanently with mental empowerment providence. There are so many cases of journalists suffering from such problems, have become not only completely free from mental problems but also too mentally empowered with the help of this advance psychological tool that is "Emotional Engineering".

8. Marriage

Marriage is the most beautiful, important, responsible and pleasant turning point in every one's life. In Indian culture, it is considered as one of the important Sanskar (the sacrament) among all 16 sacraments. The Hindi version of marriage is WIVAH (fookg = fo+okg) that means conceding responsibility specially. Therefore, it is necessary that it is accepted as in very that form as important, responsible, beautiful and in every type of pleasure as it is conceptualized through which it could determined to ensure the natural flow of endless love, mutual trust, devotion and other feelings between couple. Marriage is not only a agreement between two individuals of opposite genders like other immature civilizations but it is establishment tuning between two emotional system through sacrament which includes many different factors and among all the mutual correlation is must and that will give empowerment to married lives ahead. In fact, this is the pleasure and thrives. The advance psychology "Emotional Engineering" is the most suitable tool at present.

The "Emotional Engineering" is far beneficial for both bride and groom towards establishing themselves in new and important relationship with more responsibilities. Since girls (bride) are emotionally soft and would have to go other home and most of house responsibilities depend on them, therefore, it is very necessary for girls (bride) to be mentally stout, strong, able, caring and reasonably alert. Having such properties, she could get success in winning trust of her Sasural (home in law) and establishing new criteria of goodness. If bride is healthy, happy then she will able to keep herself away from all physical and mental problems. This is not necessary for her and own family but also better for coming baby. Because mental health of mother profoundly matters in concerns of mental and physical health of baby. Therefore, using "Emotional Engineering" before about 6 months of marriage is quite beneficial for brides towards mental empowerment. On other hand, it keeps bride away from all mental problems, which are so common these days and may be in future as well. In side-by-side she gets rid completely problems off if suffering from related to marriage and otherwise.

As far as the grooms concerned going to get married, the "Emotional Engineering" is far useful them also. It is often seen grooms are having some inappropriate extreme point of view towards brides in either positive or negative. This way their pleasure of their married life starts affected. The responsibility of making pleasant relationship is not only on solders of bride but also on an equal responsibility of grooms, there is high requirement of balanced and empowered mind to the grooms and regarding marriage related other problem "Emotional Engineering" is very useful to resolve with providence of mental empowerment. Its established fact that only empowered, able wise couple can give intelligent, smart, powerful and robust baby birth. This way we serve not ourselves but also nation and we will empower the coming generation as well.

The most mean vogue "Divorce" is not a part of our Indian culture but as on gradual adaption of foreign tongue, life style, living style and costumes our intelligence and emotional system is getting deteriorated which results increment in divorce cases in Indian society. There are so many psychological reasons behind this but the most significant and important reason is deterioration of emotional system in people. Some of people are deteriorated first some of them will later. Such social shocking mishaps can be stopped easily with the help of "Emotional Engineering".

About 8 years ago, a girl was mentally empowered through the "Emotional Engineering" before her marriage and after she established new criteria through her goodness using empowered mind and became most lovable member of her Sasural. After marriage, her husband got 6 promotions and became the youngest general manager in his working MNC. She has two very intelligent children and both of them awarded of best student every year ever since start of schooling.

A girl was suffering from fear of marriage (gamophobia) and personality disorder. She was under psychiatric medication since 1.5 years. Rather than having benefits, case became more worsening. After getting mental empowerment through "Emotional Engineering" she became completely okay with one month, there is no need of any sort of psychiatric medication to her, and in next month, her mind became so empowered to teach children in tuition. She is spending fantastic life now days.

9.   Solution of problem of children (5 to 14 years) and Development by Betterment of Parenting

As on coming changes in society, the worthless competitive property with pomp and show in people are gradually growing along. Nuclear families are coming in shape by breaking joint families. A special type of social fabric is developing and process is in special contexts of money for surviving orientation. In side-by-side due to worthless competition, speedy meeting of getting ahead and lack of sacraments influenced badly on holistic development of children. The change results lack of sacraments in children, lack of life values, lack of feeling etc. in children, which are must of being in any person ahead. Well according to various studies on child development, the fact came out that the development of children completely depends on behavior of parents and circumstances. It means children are made only from home and are deteriorated from very home. If all is well in home on behavioral ground then it is certain that development of child will be holistically fantastic and child will be a responsible and intelligent citizen of the nation, a history creator or both.

If a child gets feared in going school, has difficulty in reading, too stubborn, no obedient, his behavior is inappropriate and has weak memory then definitely there is problem which needs to solve as soon as possible through suitable and appropriate parenting with the help of "Emotional Engineering". Regarding this concern, all three are required to get mentally empowered father, Mother and Child. As parent brings changes in their behavior, the developmental changes in child come as well and gradually child goes to holistic mental empowerment with improved intelligence within 28 days in ideal conditions and generally it may take hardly 1.5 to 2 months.

About 4 years ago a case of child of 11 year old came to me of severe school phobia. He was under psychiatric medication since 3 years. Due to high level of anxiety he came in grip of gastric problem and even after prolonged treatment when he was even not right, he was advised to consult psychiatrist. Then no benefit to him by psychiatry, he came to me lastly. Using graphological research analysis of all three, I found problem in behavior of mother. As being the only son, the matter was quite emotional. Regarding mental empowerment and ridding his off the problem of school phobia as well I gave appropriate advice to parent (Both father and mother). Actually that child was anxiety ridden just due to behavior of mother. After just 1.5 month child became completely cured with full of mental empowerment and intelligence as well. After that, he did not secure less than 90% marks in any exam. The fact comes out that every child has unique personality apart from his parent's personality so the behavior of parents must according to child.

About 6 year ago, a case of hyperactive child of a Bengali couple came to me. The child so hyperactive that even 5 minutes sitting was not possible for him. Because of full lack of attentiveness and proper consistency, there was big problem in sitting for reading which results poor performance in school and ultimately child dropped out. The couple took treatment from international (psychologist was sitting in Kolkata and London as well) level psychologists and psychiatrist about 3 years but there was no benefits of that to the child. With the help of advance form of psychology "Emotional Engineering", child was become completely cured with proper intelligence. There was another case of same type of south Indian family, their child was also became cured with full mental empowerment. The "Emotional Engineering" is quite beneficial in both as a preventive measure and in curing illnesses, which is mental empowerment as well.

10. In Solving Adjustment Problem in Housewives

Nowadays in housewives problem of adjustment with other family members in addition to her husband are gradually increasing. There are so many cultural, social and value factors behind this serious problem but the most serious significant cause is behavioral problem. Well, many people are blaming TV serials for such serious social problem. They may be right on their own place but due to this the environment of home is getting affected badly, sweetness of relationship is disappearing gradually, the holistic development of person is also getting affected that increases stress problem in people that leads to many types of mental and physical problems, deteriorating mental health of family and society as well. All these problems are just due to adjustment problem of housewives. In fact this is chain of problems is also directly affecting holistic development of children. The "Emotional Engineering" has the solution of this problem through the mental empowerment just because of having micro-level diagnostic system of personality. Then our mind works on "All or None" theory that permits exact data to be given to mind towards mental empowerment, otherwise on giving excess data mind will confuse or mind will refuse lesser data as required. The confusion and process of refusing data are much more dangerous for mental and physical health.

About 7 years ago a case came to of married women from Mumbai. That woman did not want to live in her Sasural (real home) with her husband at any cost. Due to this act from her side rest of family members of both sides (bride and groom) were in high stress including her husband. Before coming to me, they had consulted many psychologists towards getting solution since very start. Both spouses came to me and woman told me that she does not like some members of her sasural. On doing her personality research, I diagnosed her having problem of behavior where as personality her husband was in right up to some extent. On diagnosing both state of mind, I made both mind learned with the help of "Emotional engineering". It took them hardly about one month. Today that woman lives in her sasural with her husband with full of joy. "Emotional Engineering" is not less than a boon who are facing problem of adjustment.

CHAPTER – 3

Method of Curing with Mental Empowerment & Communication Quotient

Method of Curing with Mental Empowerment

In fact, writing and reading are even very concrete, visible and clear Intrapersonal Communication. As handwriting deciphers complete emotional mechanism, any individual can be engineered towards cure with mental empowerment through perfect medium. Intrapersonal communication is a very vast area through which a human being learns towards better living means skillful living. The specific skill makes ground for development for "survival of the fittest". Everything whatever is visible (in all aspects directly and indirectly both), sensible, living or nonliving, provokes us for communication directly or indirectly. The living and sensitive being cannot be remaining without being affected with all what are in circumstances. What type of communication goes on in our while coming in touch by any mean of things or factors, this all depend upon what format of emotional system we have after sensing before by communication. Therefore, on my opinion the Intrapersonal communication is "what type of and what perception goes on while observing a subject or object". The interpersonal communication is a small part of Intrapersonal Communication occurs through verbal communication between two individuals. Besides being of all factors during interpersonal communication, the maximum part of verbal communication of interpersonal communication insists individuals for intrapersonal communication and then he starts considering all objects as subject from he is being communicated. At the time interpersonal communication, the two way of communication take place one is verbal and other one is intrapersonal communication that considers infinite factors related to person by any mean and according to unique personality on unique emotional mechanism.

There is very deep correlation between intrapersonal communication and handwriting. Whatever an individual gets from his circumstances through perception of conditional factors, initially all make its own base in mind separately. Even if they all come together in mind this way but make own base differently. Moreover, later, the individual responds conditional factors on very these bases to get effects and after effects. The effects then go to under evaluation how they are to develop with pleasure. This is process gets repeats repeatedly regarding different-same things, events or both. The specific intrapersonal communications converts into personality traits through this process. Personality is a process continuous throughout life with learning every moment. That is why it is told that a man even learns art of living at the time of death.

As human being writes with reflex action that is why handwriting is affected by all what is going on in mind and its state of mind as well. Now any two handwriting could not be same like any two personality could not be same. This is because of different way and form of intrapersonal communication form conditional factors and circumstances. Forms of responses and to respond the subject according to form of mental status of individuals are clearly revealed by handwriting and with fluctuations going on in mind. Thus, through handwriting we can easily reach to the state of mind, which is personality. Analyzing handwriting, we can get even minute change comes in mind comes through any conditional factor via intrapersonal communication.

Making of Therapeutic Handwriting Analysis Personality Research Report for Specific and adequate Intrapersonal Communication

All mental illnesses take place because of Intrapersonal miscommunications. Therefore, to cure, there is very strong natural way through which illness comes that is mental empowerment using perfect and adequate Intrapersonal communication according to unique personality. In fact specific intrapersonal communication get converted into personality traits and just through which we can reform or create personality traits via brain learning to the neural pathways of personality traits. This is "Emotional Engineering" the method towards curing with "mental empowerment". As it is mentioned earlier that without proper mental empowerment, no one could be cured. Because of working on "all or none" theory, it is very necessary to give proper data to be communicated intarpersonally to create or reform new neural pathways of different required traits according to the unique personality and requirements as well. By reading at least twice a day (not more than three times) and practicing specific doodles mind starts learning. To bring even a small change in personality, it is must to overhaul whole personality with keeping all emotional system with correlation accordingly. Therefore, only this way the mind and ultimately whole personality of any person can be engineered.

Emotional Engineering = Therapeutic Personality Research Report for intrapersonal communication + Set of Graphotherapies to make appropriate communicated data

Therapeutic personality research report is understanding emotional mechanism through micro level handwriting analysis of unique personality of a individual on active personality traits, providing consulting guidance as per exact demand of personality neither more nor less, keeping tracked by "all or none" theory in on which mind and nervous system work. To avoid the effect of rejection on more than required data given while on being confused given data less than required.

On practicing Given graphotherapies 4-6 times a day, person's mind becomes started learning properly towards curing through "mental empowerment". There is no need of making report on all 127 traits, as there will be too much data to make mind confuse that may be dangerous. To prepare the therapeutic research report it should be sorted only active traits out according to the unique personality, which may vary between 15–40 in number. These all sorting should be based on emotional mechanism and graphotherapies should be given according to demand of unique handwriting as unique personality. Thereafter, report should be prepared with remedies according to the demand of personality. No two therapeutic research reports can be exactly same because no two personalities are same.

It is must for client towards curing to read therapeutic research report twice a day whole with practicing set of graphotherapies 4 – 6 times a day. Incomplete reading and practicing will not be effective. There are some important should be kept under mind of clients –

(i)   Therapeutic personality research report must have to be read completely to communicate all data at a time and practiced set of graphotherapies whole at a time.

(ii)   Due period of following by reading and practicing as well is 1 month. Leaving practice in mid-term may be harmful.

(iii) Extreme or over practice must have to be avoided.

There are many properties of mental disorders-stricken clients may be commonly occurred in most of disorder-stricken people that should keep in mind at the time of preparing handwriting analysis based therapeutic personality research report understanding "emotional mechanism". It may be possible that any or many properties are missing in person so, those one should not be mentioned in therapeutic research report. Well, characteristics of most of the properties are given but as characteristics are observed in handwriting changes should be brought in report accordingly.

Here there is a very important fact that must be kept in mind that preparation therapeutic personality report strictly must be in mother language, in layman's language, must be legible and able to get as well, because in mother language the whole mind of person remains 100% active while in foreign tongue it reduces by just around 1-5%. Meaning is clear, foreign tongue is in fact good for nothing regarding "mental empowerment".

Therefore, towards empowerment and curing we just need complete active mind rather than little bit. The data provided by "Mastishk Anusandhan Kendra, Gurgaon, India" during research on language in 2009. So, towards curing and empowering mind foreign tongue must be avoided.

Communication Quotient (Comm. Q.)

Communication Quotient is a score based on very basic concept that is communication. Communication Quotient is very simple method through which we can know the level of mental disorders. Communication is very raw substance that builds whole personality. That is why using it, we can score the level of all mental disorders.

Communication Quotient stands for mental disorders rather than mental empowerment and mental health. With the help of this equation, we cannot know how much a person has mental health. As it is stated earlier that according to Sigmond Freud all disorders are caused by external stimulus, it directly means that causing stimuli are in fact communication. That is why on communication level we can level intensity of disorders. However, form of communication varies according to circumstances but some value of are universally fixed.

Communication Quotient (Comm. Q.) is "ratio of the given input command to the person and output response coming from person".

Comm. Q. = Output Response / Input Command

Person has "normal mental health" when its value is **1** or around it. Such people are "Normal and Reasonable Communicator."

More than 1 value -

Its value is more than 1 first "Anxiety disorder" second "Personality disorder" and "Schizophrenic" person has its value Infinity respectively. People with this disorder are "Hyper communicator."

Anxiety, Personality Disorder or Schizophrenia > 1

Less than 1 value –

Its Value is less than 1 first "Dissociative Disorder" second "Mood Disorder" and lastly "death" has its value Zero respectively. People with this disorder are "Hypo communicator."

Dissociative, Mood Disorder or Death < 1

On this basis of Communication Quotient, we can divide mental disorders in to two clear wings, one is "Right-wing mental disorders" includes Anxiety, Personality Disorder and Schizophrenia has more value than 1 which stands for normal and healthy person and other one is "Left-wing mental Disorders" includes Dissociative, and Mood Disorders has lesser value than 1.

Right-wing Disorders   –   Hyper Communicator

Left-wing Disorders   –   Hypo Communicator

Normal   –   Normal and Reasonable Communicator

In case of psychosomatic disorders outputs responses are internal, which occurs within the body and only individual can feel.

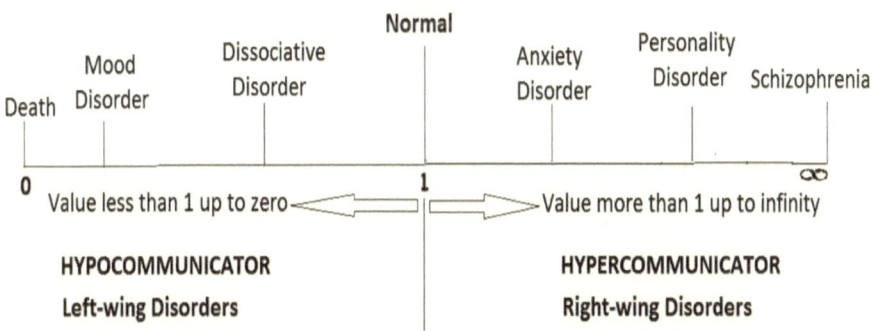

Fig. Ch 3.1 Diagram of Communication Quotient

The value of Communication Quotient zero, one and infinity is universally common for all people for dead, normal healthy and schizophrenic person respectively. Dead body does not respond on giving infinite commands, it means score of Communication Quotient is **"Zero"**. On the contrary, schizophrenic person has score value **"infinity"** because they only respond without giving command. Normal and healthy person responds reasonably, on only what command he is given, nothing more and nothing less than reasonable requirement that is why normal person has value of Communication Quotient placed **"One"**. Whereas, other values may be vary according to culture, country, circumstances and tolerance of body also. Well, I did not test scientifically this theory on people but suppose it would be better scale towards knowing level of seriousness of mental disorders. Because of "Communication Quotient" all personality can be scored personality successfully regarding behavior, cognitive concerns, potential and others.

These days, multiple disorders are commonly observed and the most common one among them is mood disorder with anxiety (depression with OCD). Communication Quotient is even applicable in scoring such multiple disorders in isolated form in reference of each other. The reason behind this is that one disorder act as stimulus for other disorder and vice-versa. At a time, only disorder should be considered and on the basis of one another disorder should be scored. Regarding psychosomatic disorders the output responses from the side of person become mostly internal as on external given external command as stimuli.

Regarding scoring communication must be in mother language, non-reactive and pleasant environment and according to individual's culture. Foreign tongue and all things that can impose even a little bit of pressure and stress must be avoided. Mother Language is very important because in this language, individual's mind remains 100% active without stress and that is why it will yield actual data.

UNIT - 1

MOOD DISORDERS

CHAPTER – 1

Depressive Disorders

Mood disorders, as it is clear by name that person has lost control on his feelings and concerned mental status regarding specific situation. The mood disorder leads unbalance in feelings and longitudinal state of mind having episodic form of "mania" and "hypomania". In this disorder, fluctuation occurs in the feelings causes as unbalanced. Simultaneously, according to the fluctuation in his feelings and emotions, person has reluctance in manic episode while in episode of hypomania has over affection with his circumstances. Due to this emotional phenomenon person cannot not adjust their normal level of mood according to situation and that ultimately phenomenon results many social and occupational problems in his life. In this type of mental disorder, the mental status of person is sometimes "depressive" and sometimes "manic". Both statuses come to the person in alternate. The badly affected emotional balance carried through out.

In DSM-IV there are three types of mood disorder are inscribed-

1. **Depressive Disorder** - It is also known as "Unipolar disorder" and its main symptom is depression and sorrow. At the same time, person lacks of hunger, sleep and loss in body weight and level of his activeness becomes very low. It is divided in to two parts –

    a. **Dysthymic Disorder** – The chromic form of depressive mood from that person has been suffering from for long time and due to that person laid under such condition for many years. "Person feels lack of interest and joy" in every condition, situation or regarding anything. Although, the person is observed normal but depressive mood is continuing effectively.

Symptoms revealed by Handwriting - Handwriting depicts clearly "dysthymic disorder" in following ways-

(i) In handwriting sample some letters look like "hanging". "Hanging letters" are distinguishing and one of the characteristic features of "depressive disorder." In any stage of life, if hanging letters are seen in handwriting, it is definite confirmation that the person is going in grip of "depressive mood.". Thus, "hanging letters are common distinguishing feature of all type of depressive disorder" The feature when in person "reluctance from life and system" takes place Because of the "shifting base" on which person depends upon, is going to be shifted.

(ii) The other symptoms are observed as in letters of handwriting sample those are "d, t, l, b, e, l, f, I, d, h, and k" are in much irregular fashion. Along with this feature, the "lower zone loops" of relevant letters like in g, j, z, f are also observed irregular. At some where these are observed normal and somewhere not with having quite different fashion of its accomplishment. This feature of handwriting stands for "emotional drive" in the person and is deciphered because of "dysthymic disorder". The emotional system becomes badly disturbed. Sometimes the person gets much more emotional and sometimes becomes highly pessimist.

(iii) Blunt "t-ends" are observed in handwriting sample. The blunt endings characteristic feature is also obvious in m, n, l, d, a, l, h, I, u, being "blunt ends" are indication of "violation" in the person. Well all types of criminals and violent people show "blunt t end" in handwriting and regarding "dysthymic disorder" it is observed as a feature in significantly which leads cruelty. Generally, if blunt t-end is not observed, they will be definitely likely to be observed in other letters. Dysthymic disorder person get himself in reactive stage due to continued irritating situations and most of conditional factors to which he is facing. Such conditions may have been prolonging to be continued for more than one year.

(iv)   Person who possesses the "base line loop" in many letters like S, D, S, P, are in irregular fashion but it is seems that he would has intention to make them. The base line loops are identification sign of intention about concern system paid by person. The abnormal fashion of making such looks is "burden of paying intention" which may come into the open as burden of responsibilities. From which person wants to get him freed eagerly. The characteristic feature also depicts the "unsuccessful efforts" being done by person against those of burden what intentions are being paid as responsibilities.

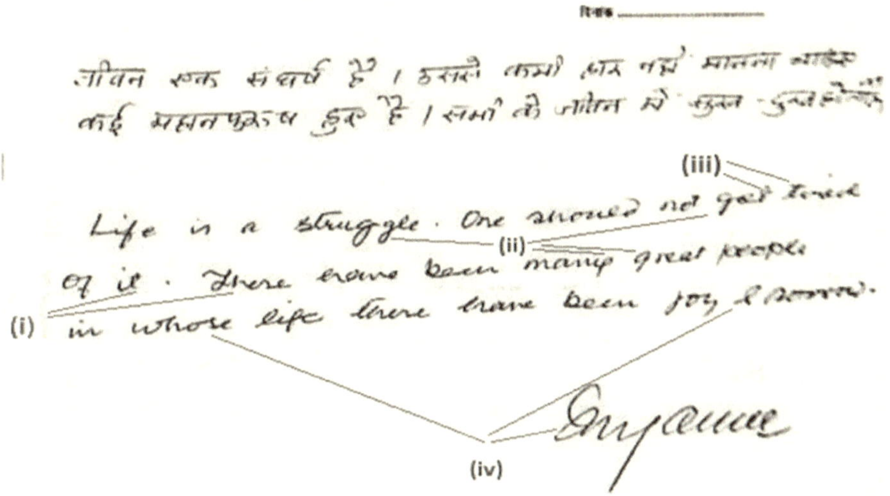

Fig. 1.1

Dysthymic Disorder – This disorder will be diagnosed as -

Hanging letters + Irregular loop in lower zone of letter + blunt t-ends + Irregular base line loops.

A. Important Traits To Be Considered Accordingly While Making Report -

Towards reforming personality traits through intrapersonal communication by neural pathways of those via brain learning, personality research report is required as mentioned earlier and to prepare therapeutic personality research report consist of all instructions to be communicated and state of mind along. There are following important traits to be considered according to the unique personality revealed by handwriting sample for communication, consulting guidance or counseling towards empowering personality traits would lead to mental empowerment with cure. Well, considering these all are not mandatory and strictly depend on what handwriting reveals, which may let permit to add new traits not mentioned here. The traits are characterized here by as handwriting depicted by chronic psychopaths. On missing any or many characteristics, change in guidance format will occur accordingly. Well during preparation of therapeutic personality research report, these following suggestions should be kept in mind. If person is on self-cure, he must prepare his therapeutic research report this way towards curing. Because of being unique personality, report will be unique so, uniqueness must be kept under deep consideration and differences should be identified according to form, presence and absence of characteristics -

1. Logically hard Determination of conditional status and condition must be avoided by person, because confidence of person on any subject or matter firstly goes down, then up and lastly becomes normal by some sort of extra efforts which is characterized in handwriting as -

   (i) Both alignment of handwriting sample and signature goes down first then up.

   (ii) Some letters are not made in homogeneous fashion

   (iii) Controversially the gaps between two successive words are not same on comparing between mother language (Hindi) and English language.

(iv) Signature is observed as slight upward going without underline.

(v) Some letters are observed changed with slight vibration and deformation.

2. Person must use normal conditional factors for communication because of sustaining logic power for long time, which is characterized by –

(i) Speed of handwriting is normal.

(ii) Letters of handwriting are not in homogeneous form.

(iii) Abnormalities are in gap between successive words.

3. Person must set smaller goal or target of his working because there are much difference occurs between target and working, characterized by –

(i) The complementary parts of letters are made too far from their origin.

(ii) Vibration and unnecessary folds are seen in handwriting.

4. Person must raise his ambition gradually because of not having high ambition and considers rather more contemporary conditional factors in context of target. This is characterized by –

(i) Handwriting and Signature both are downward going uniformly.

(ii) Signature is often found not underlined.

(iii) There is unclear and incomplete signature.

(iv) Signature covers normal area.

5. Person must take hard and obstinate stand on some matters his obstinacy must not be hidden as he does not have proper strong obstinacy and due to not acting properly person has problem of recognition. This is characterized in handwriting as –

(i) Shape of letters is smaller in handwriting where as not in signature.

(ii) Usually signature covers normal area.

(iii) Very slight upward going signature.

(iv) Words and letters are not well furnished.

6. Person must make his ego strong because normally peak negative ego becomes one of the main properties. Which is characterized in handwriting as -

(i) Letters of handwriting are much smaller than signature.

(ii) Handwriting goes downward first.

(iii) Gap between successive words in English sample observed more than normal.

7. Enjoying every condition for the person is necessary because happiness is affected negative way by conditional factors and concepts as well as being not availability of new condition which is depicted by handwriting as –

(i) Handwriting is in manic form

(ii) Not being of proper uphill slants in handwriting, which may be in signature.

(iii) Normally signature goes down first then up.

8. In case of utilizing things, person must have all option open regarding that concern as much as he can because of lacking proper method of utilizing that particular thing using concepts from ambition with having proper variation, characterized by handwriting as –

(i) No proper elevation in handwriting with deformation in letters.

(ii) Signature is slight upward going.

(iii) Relevant letters are found almost complete and closed

(iv) Speed of handwriting is slow whereas speed of signature is rather high in comparison to handwriting.

(v) Very slight amount of deformation is observed in handwriting.

9. There should be new fields to expand for the person because there is lack of ability in person to look for new area for expansion depicted in handwriting as-

   (i) Signature does not cover considerably big area.
   (ii) There is no marking in signature.
   (iii) Upper zone of signature also does not covers bigger area in comparison to lower area.
   (iv) There is more width of letters in comparison to that of length.

10. Being extrovert unnecessarily for the person would be harmful because of due to mood disorder and reluctance he becomes quiet more introvert which is depicted by handwriting as-

    (i) Most of letters are closed except some are open.
    (ii) Words begin from different levels.
    (iii) Gap between two successive letters gradually becomes lesser as termination comes near.
    (iv) Somewhere signature goes down first then up.
    (v) Signature has slight vibration.

11. There should be specific stage for accommodation to the person because person looks forward about happening and incomplete accommodation with changeable concepts. In handwriting it is depicted as –

    (i) The letters of words are interconnected with each other in specific style.
    (ii) Letters of words are incomplete at many places in handwriting sample.

12. If necessary person should go for time bound compromise as obstinacy is not properly stronger to take stand on particular matter which is depicted in handwriting as –

    (i) There are more circular folds in handwriting.
    (ii) There is no proper elevation in handwriting and signature.

13. Maintaining dairy would be more beneficial for the person towards curing because person does not have proper form of self presentation when handwriting does not show –

    (i)   No shield made by elongation or extension of letters.
    (ii) No out growth is observed at the end of signature.

14. Conclusion of project run by person is very necessary because conclusion of any work provides big satisfaction with ability but person does not feel it properly as his works remains endless. This is depicted by handwriting as –

    (i)   All letters of handwriting are not completed in same manner as well as the terminations of sentences have completion so far.

15. On suspicion person should not react until getting proof because of having strong reaction on apprehension. This is revealed in handwriting as –

    (i)   Letters of handwriting are comparatively small.
    (ii) Signature is not underline.
    (iii) At starting point of signature loop is observed.
    (iv) Segmentation in words is observed in gradual increasing order.
    (v)   Gap among two words is lesser in mother language (Hindi) than that of English.

16. Using artistry would be more beneficial for the person because of having comparatively better sense of it but due to being that unused person stayed denied of it. This is depicted by handwriting as –

    (i)   Manic form of handwriting
    (ii) Proper pressure of pen created on the paper
    (iii) Normal speed of handwriting.

17. Avoiding loneliness is necessary for the person because of reluctance from circumstances and conditions are common in the person which is depicted in handwriting as –

    (i)   Long down stroke is observed in handwriting sample.

    (ii)   Big loop may be occurred in lower zone

    (iii)   Hanging letters are found at many places in handwriting.

    (iv)   There may be long strokes in upper zone.

18. Person should avoid imposing his thoughts on others and he must not pass orders regarding any context instead of this he must give more and more options to break stereotyped blockage of mind on level of thoughts. This is depicted in handwriting as –

    (i)   First letter of signature forms loop

    (ii)   There are many letters in handwriting have both acute and circular folds.

    (iii)   Letters of handwriting are smaller than signature.

19. Person should write his thought down in a dedicated note book and on fix time interval he should recall all because there is trait of coming new thoughts in the person which must be used properly. This is revealed by handwriting as –

    (i)   Letters are poorly elevated at somewhere.

    (ii)   Speed of handwriting slightly more than normal.

    (iii)   Irregular gap between two successive words is irregular in handwriting sample.

20. Person should not miss the opportunity to meet new people to break loneliness and stereotyped mind. This is revealed in handwriting as –

    (i)   There is needle extension in upper zone.

    (ii)   Letters of signature are poorly wider.

    (iii)   Small loops are seen in upper zone of letters like h, b, f etc.

Graphotherapies – On diagnosing dysthymia on symptoms as shown above following graphotherapies are able to apply to cure the person. These are helpful in reforming the distorted neural pathways of concerning disorder –

(i)   Person does not need to determine his conditional status through conditional factors logically hard because confidence of person depends upon many conditional factors that are why it is in fluctuating form. Commonly it becomes firstly up then down which is characterized in handwriting by going up slightly then down. At the same time, some letters of handwriting are observed changed either deformed with having some sort of vibrations, additional deformations or with both. Therefore, to remove it the following doodle should be given to the person to practice –

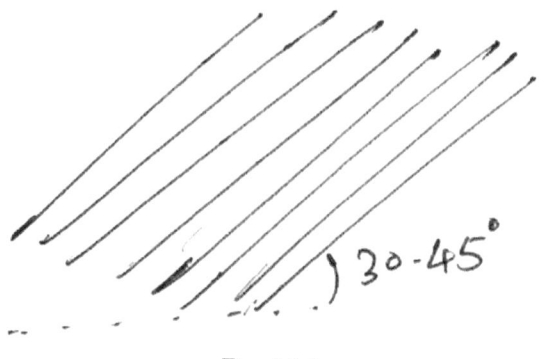

Fig. 1.1.i

"The upward going slanted lines on white paper should be practiced by person for 4-6 times a day just for 2-5 minutes. The angle of slant should be in between 30-45°. The speed of drawing the lines should be increasing gradually day by day. Formation of new neural pathways of personality traits depends upon the speed of writing.

(ii)   The 'upward going slanted lines are responsible for clearing 'ambition' in the person which is not used on strong logical definition. Strong and clear ambition having person does not pay strong intention on normal running matters conditional factors, events, conditions, situation or subjects causes turning out depressive mood. Clear and strong ambition makes own strong emotional system towards the goal. Imagination of ambition would be pleasant but the process not.

To make person pleasant the process, following graphotherapy should be prescribed to the person to practice –

Fig. 1.1.ii

"Upward going slanted connected 'u' on 30-45°. The speed of drawing should be high or gradual increasing for 4-6 times a day for 2-5 minutes. It should mind that there must not be loop on connection.

(iii) Person should use normal conditional factors for communication because logic power does not sustain for long time as having irregular speed of handwriting. The symptom is characterized by normal speed of handwriting, letters of handwriting do not found in homogeneous fashion and gap among words is seen in irregular fashion observed more than normal and somewhere seen lesser than that of. Due to irregular gap there is conflict occurred between two traits i.e. condition born mental overlapping and condition born mental disownity. Therefore to adapt such trait person must have to go for following changes in his handwriting as –

a. Person has to slow his handwriting and signature speed.

Fig. 1.1.iii.a

b. Gap among towards must be regular.

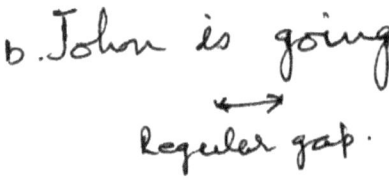

Fig. 1.1.iii.b

c. Letters have to make clear, homogenous and complete e.g.

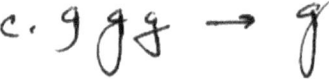

Fig. 1.1.iii.c

d. Do not make downward going end of word, sentences and letters. e. g. Fig.

Fig. 1.1.iii.d

(iv)   Normally it is found that person wants to achieve many and bigger goals or compelled by someone or some conditional factor (s), which would be quite beyond his capacity. Such types of conditions directly affect person's personality in a way that person tries to meet out target or goal as a big necessary keeping that on his top priority but that becomes a burden to which he cannot get freed. This is negative impact of the goal. Generally, such problem arises while person is not able to do his efforts towards achieving the goal systematically. Here steps should be determined on priority ground according to personality. To remove this problem person has to get into the habit of stepwise working regarding achievement of his goal. It should be noted here that in reference of a goal number of steps of his efforts should not be exceeded more than 5. The ideal number is 3 to 5. As I have found this fact from handwriting of world's most wanted terrorist Osama bin Laden. In handwriting "burden goal" is characterized by the complementary parts of letters are observed much in context of his origin unnecessary vibration and unnecessary acute folds.

Towards curing this problem person should work additionally on to achieve some smaller goal, having small campaigns, which must be time bounded and under strict control of person regarding proceedings. Person should go for practicing some graphotherapy which are as follows-

a.   Complementary parts of words must be attached to the "body" l. g. i-dot t-bar, x j or at exact place

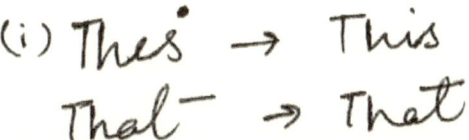

(i) Thes → This
Thal → That

Fig. 1.1.iv.a

b. To divide the campaign in various steps, the person should practice the dotted lines for 2-5 minutes and 4-6 times a day.

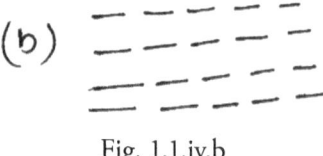

Fig. 1.1.iv.b

c. It is necessary that person could find the meaningful and worthy factors in most of conditions. It had better that person is provided many meaningful and worthy factors in selective from. Such processes inspire the person to come on "priority-management" and through this phenomenon even the "time-management" vice-versa. Indeed an instant valuation of complete conditions and factors run at a time. Person should practice it 4-6 time a day for 2-5 minutes. Shape should not be smaller.

(c) + + + + I^{st} step → |
+ + + + IInd step → —
+ + + +

Fig. 1.1.iv.c

(v) Person should not go for infinite activation form on any subject or topic. All campaign of various topics and subjects should have impact according to their own format. During continuity, the person should react according to the subjects. New courses of thought and mode of thinking may come under consideration by this process. Person should stop on particular subject for definite time.

For this purpose person should practice following doodle for 4-6 times a day for 2-5 minutes.

Fig. 1.1. v

It has to be practiced with slow speed and with intention that it is just more than dot and less than line.

(vi) After completing one campaign, the person needs to look for another goal with proper valuation. The valuation is procedure to recall to all concerned happenings, events, condition and situations related to the subject and some sort of relevant factors for proper valuation according to the contemporary need or requirements.

Regarding this concern to set all neural pathways, following doodles play significant role for proper stimulation related to concerning traits regarding this mental disorder as well

Fig. 1.1 vi

Mode of practice is as such as before

(vii) For campaign and thought, person needs proper activeness. It may vary according to the campaign. To do well on campaign person needs following doodle to practice.

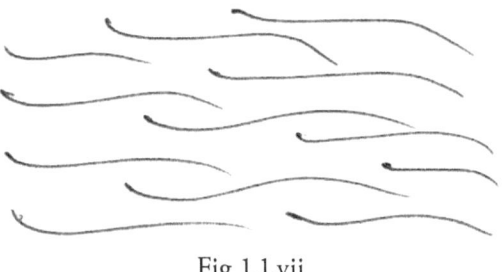

Fig 1.1.vii

(viii) In person with depressive mood disorder, it is normally found that ambition is not as clear to achieve the particular goal with no other ambition like other emotional factors are seen in "saturation stage". It is very necessary for the person to come out of this stage on priority because of being saturation stage as having intention to change mode of perception by change in mechanism of perception with the help of its all related factors remain in composite form may be any type of social, economic, personality or academic related. To come out of this stage, person has to make either new ambition or raise his ambition according to his personality. This is the "inside warded saturation stage" which is characterized in the handwriting as handwriting and signature both are not uniformly upward going. Such phenomenon depicts clearly that no more high ambition observed in the person that would be more than contemporary status.

There are two graphotherapies to insure coming out of this saturation stage emotional system due to which person is not able to think better about understandings of related circumstances system to get more conditional factors according to his personal requirements would have to be helpful in emotional thrive of the person -

(a) This is composed of two if two figures one is high speed drown upward lines which should be started from bottom and other one is small circles which should made under the drawn line is perpendicular area from upper side to down and in right side. Circles should make with slow speed.

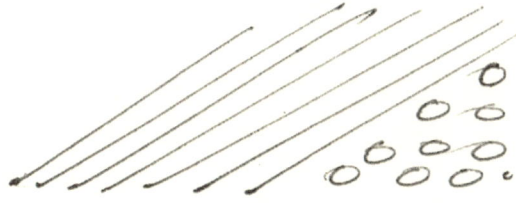

Fig. 1.1.viii.a

b. The dysthimic person have to keep some sort of "investigative trait" or "analytical trait" that can be developed on "peak navigation of fundamental personality traits" to analyze his ambition, its form and mode of self-establishment accordingly in any particular condition or in overall circumstances. Regarding process of analysis, investigation provides many factors for getting adopted accordingly as per requirements. Such factors play very important role in creating opportunities for further development.

Regarding this type of abnormal person, it generally found that they have incomplete and distorted form of "investigation trait" which results only strong negative outputs as well as infers negative conditional factors and due to which the person get depressed and gradually going on towards in grip of dysthimia. To make person complete (positive and negative both), it is necessary to create the "analytical or investigative trait" as in active stage of this trait person should be more and more expressive. It is possible if he goes for proper debate on particular matter as per his likings.

At the same time, it is necessary to practice following graphotherepies irregularly but gap must not be exceeded more than 7 days and it must not be given if symptoms of anxiety are shown by handwriting and signature.

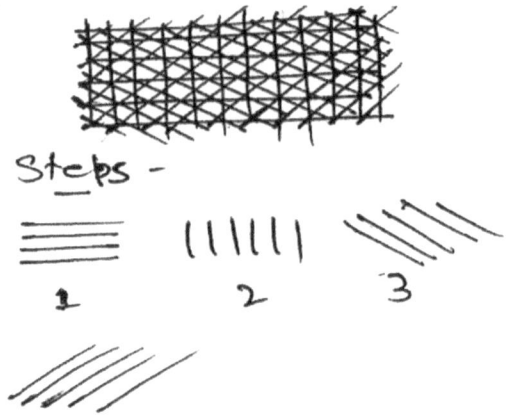

Fig. 1.1.viii.b

Lines must be extremely denser as it could be as possible. It has to be practiced with slow speed. Regarding each therapy, time should be taken not less than 90 seconds.

(ix) Persons who are suffering from dysthymic disorder do not have appropriate obstinacy due to blurred and opaque picture of his ambition that leads to goal of life. The clear ambition having concepts makes its own 'achieving system' in perspective of goal. If obstinacy in such a way that to give proper recognition gets it shaped automatically likewise appropriate obstinacy possessing person can make his proper 'goal achieving system' provided having clear ambition. Therefore, it is quite necessary to make obstinacy strong according to ambitions that should be in proper expressive form through which the person creates his own self-accountabilies.

Normally such person do not possesses his strong acting from which is characterized in the handwriting by shape of letters in handwriting is smaller where as not in signature, words and letters are not well furnished and signature covers normal area.

To improve or make strong the obstinacy in dysthymic disorder suffering person, there are two traits in strong from there are two graphotherapies as follows

a. **Strong obstinacy** - To do it strong the practice of following doodle is necessary. About this concern a point must be noted that, it should be prospective, so the end must be in upright direction from the origin.

   Both of there must be practiced according to previous doodles.

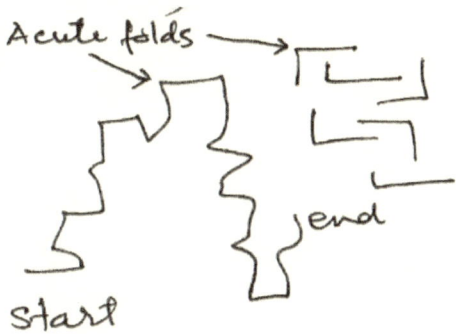

Fig. 1.1. ix.a

a. More Factors Considering Strong Proud, to do this trait properly strong, the letters should be some wider and bigger. The width of letters plays important role. Consideration of more factors keeps person in continuation process for long time on some subjects. Following doodle is important to strong this trait.

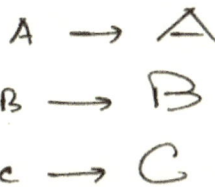

Fig. 1.1.ix.b

Simultaneously, more width of letter plays important role in keeping person happier by providing many conditional factors. Therefore, Stress causing factors could be easily come under control of dysthymic person. More width of letter intends to consider many types of factors more and more but person by nature, will select only those of happiness causing factors on correlation with many other traits. After formation of neural pathways of such traits, even on invasion of deep sorrow causing factors/condition the person could easily manage towards turning those into happiness. The given doodle should be practiced sometimes instead of regularly.

(x) Healthy Ego is a one of the important trail plays role to maintain the status of behavior. Because of lacking it person feels difficulties in affirmation on any subject and determination of his priorities. In the case of dysthymic disorder person, the person does not have prospective view on the subject and have very short-term options of his working on particularity. Such options come from contemporary factors, which would be conditional or person born. Due to being negative approach a particular subject and reluctance from life, the person feels much difficulty to be affirmed on that particular subject. It is must to make the person affirmed and determine him priorities according to time demand.

Normally dysthymic person are extremely sensitive towards satisfy his ego. All activities regarding such satisfaction procedure produce pessimism. In their initial stages these are produced due to activity on any one topic, later on it expends on other subjects and ultimately the person becomes completely pessimist and dysthymic. The handwriting depicts the unhealthy ego by the sizes of letters observed in about similar possessed by handwriting and signature whereas size of letters of handwriting are smaller than those of signature then there is a controversy in dysthymic personality having person.

To make strong the ego, the first letter of word should be made very big in comparison of other letters in having appropriation in relevant letters. e. g.

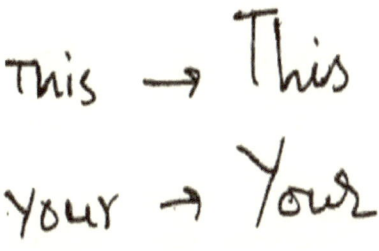

Fig. 1.1. x

(xi) It is found that dysthymic person has reluctance from proper "method of using of different thing" due to lack of option about that. The person looks for only in that direction or method of utilizing thing which are available to him and have been used in past. The method, which is being used by him, does not correlate with him ambition born concepts which is characterized in handwriting with some specified deformation in handwriting and speed of handwriting more than signature.

Such person should have more and more options of utilization of things. Methods of utilization should be kept under testing and change to get some now opportunities for stimulating the formation of new pathways.

There are four doodles as graphotherapies for creating more and more options for utilizing things-

a. it should draw with slow speed for 2-5 minutes.

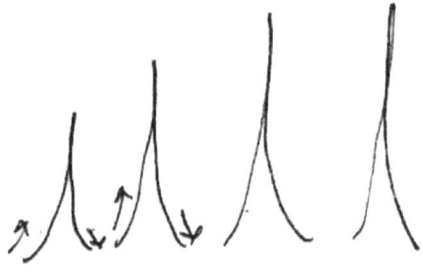

Fig. 1.1. xi.a

b. This is responsible for doing extra efforts towards achieving extra highness on utilization method of anything. It should be practiced with normal speed for 2-5 minutes daily.

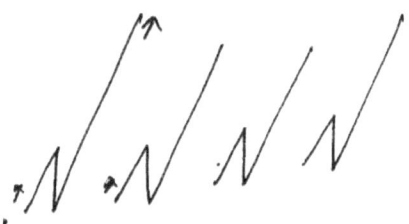

Fig. 1.1.xi.b

c. The "Slant arrow head" which is irresponsible for utilizing present and this is responsible for utilizing conditional factors with proper prospect. It should be practiced with high speed must not with slow speed.

Fig. 1.1.xi.c

d. This is responsible to insist the intention to look forward for new creative methods regarding utilization things. It should be practiced with high speed for 2-5 minutes. These is a point of mind in this doodle is the second body is elevated and ended deeply i.e. the baseline cross should be on half.

Fig. 1.1.xi.d.

(xii) The dysthymic persons have some extra need of exaggeration on particular subject in some sort of abnormal way to better sense of his circumstances, situations and related condition instead of overall behavioral. As normally, they are introvert in which condition the intention of exaggeration creates anomaly in his conduct and behavior. Therefore, he starts the efforts to communicate however with responding the results of his exaggerated conducts. In handwriting such symptoms depicted by most of letters of handwriting are closed whereas some are open, many of letters are completed anyhow and not in same fashion, signature goes downward first tern upwards slightly and signature has slight vibration.

The exaggeration from of extroversion is an abnormal status. It would beneficial if communication goes on worth fully. This is why the contemporary target will be clear as person expects from situation then goes to consider all related conditional factors along. Therefore, there is only one graphotherapy to overcome the anomaly regarding this trait.

I^st step   -   a draw a circle

IInd step   -   Then draw bar just upper side of circle, it should be

It should be practiced with slow speed for 2 to 5 minutes for 5-10 times daily

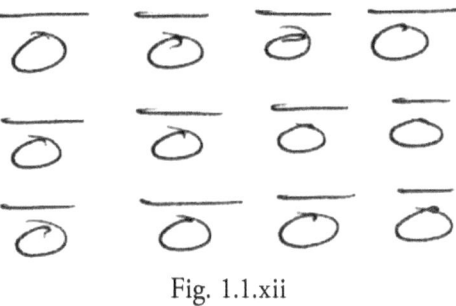

Fig. 1.1.xii

(xiii) The trait of thoughtfulness in dysthymic persons is observed in pervaded form but with lack of definite pattern due to which sometimes it is strongly activated and sometimes disappears. Therefore, mind could stimulate badly on emotional level and on other hand there is possibility, which directly disturb the mode of perception. All emotional matters and subjects come under consideration of the person in exact better way according to his personal requirements. Because of this emotional phenomenon a sequel of understanding efforts from inferior level takes place.

Such symptoms are reflected by handwriting as the upper zone loop in h, l, d, b, f, and t is not seen in some fashion. Somewhere it is seen wider and some where needle extension without having loop.

To make rid person off this abnormalities in thoughtfulness, the dysthymic person must not has to miss any opportunities to meet new people and creates new area of his sociality with high scope. There is only one graphotherapy to improve this trait. Signature must be in two segments.

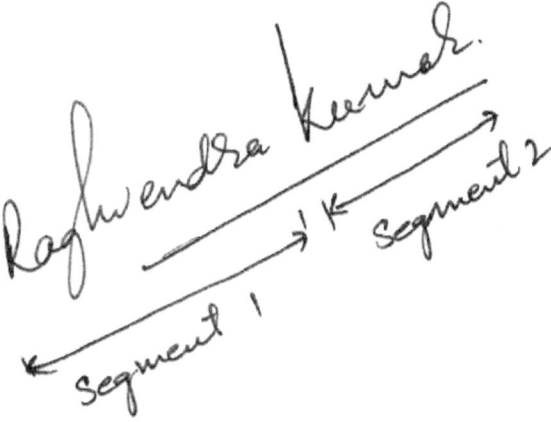

Fig. 1.1.xiii

Chapter – 2

Depression

Depression is not a disorder that may be just a normal reaction of certain life events. It may be resulted as symptom of side effect of medication. The meaning of depression is sadness produced in mood or a clinical syndrome which is composed of five types of symptoms i.e. emotional, motivational, behavioral, cognitive and somatic, called clinical depression. Instead of depressive mood, clinical depression is diagnosed as possessing other symptoms like tiredness, lack of power, disturbance is sleep, lack of consistency, lack hunger etc.

Depression has some significant emotional symptoms. People suffering from depression have sadness hopelessness, guilt feeling idleness etc. Out of all symptoms the most common symptom is sadness. In depression, with sadness, anxiety is also observed in prominent form these days. Family, entertainment, sex, hungers all things sound worthless to such people. Most of those people do not have interest in their lives. Reluctance from life is one of the most common symptoms of acute depression.

Generally, a depressed person either has negative attitude or lack of attitude drive about himself, his future and related circumstances. In connection of his negative thinking as he feels that significantly results lack of self esteem, guilt feeling, self responsibility of his unsuccessful regarding any context and self incompatibility gradually his feelings about intellectual ability decreases day by day and confusion increases simultaneously.

At the same time, depressed person poses his interest in daily routine works. Lack of drive, spontaneity and initiative are also found in most of depressed person. They are forcibly compelled to maintain their social conduct as well as relations, to go for sexual relationships with partner, to take need and to talk. These all symptoms are categorized under motivational symptoms.

About all functions of depressed persons are found in drastic decreasing order. They work but in improper way. They like loneliness. Such person walks slowly, which seems that neither they want to walk nor they have power to do. Their speeches and with cast are downplay. These are symptoms categorized under behavioral syndrome.

Headache, panic sensation in chest, constipation, indigestion, and pain in whole body occur in depressed person. Such people suffer from tiredness which remains sustained abnormally for long duration. According to Ballneger (1998) about 9% people suffer from hypersommia.

Symptoms revealed by Handwriting – The handwriting depicts depression by having following features-

(i) Unlike dysthymic disorder, the depressive disorder possesses two or more than two letter in sequence in some words, observed as hanging form in handwriting sample. The symptom depicts the deep impact of depression caused by various depending factors of personality on that personality itself depends on, seen in handwriting due to strong "reluctance from all vivid factors that is life " than dysthymic disorder. At the time of attack the person gets more active towards reluctance. This is one of the significant features of depressive mood disorder.

(ii) The g, y, g, z, have big loop or without loop. The symptoms reveal the negative attitude in the depressed person. In handwriting simple the g with big loop and without loop are observed somewhere but not commonly and in rhythmic fashion. Pessimism is resulted by negative attitude that is either being not succeeded in achieving the goal or feeling as incompatible for that particular situation. Goal determined by his ambition therefore, in depressed person signature reveals some high ambition i.e. upward going signature may be with underline. The g loop is characterized almost commonly same in handwriting and signature.

(iii)   In confidence, there is fluctuation observed in alignment of handwriting. Handwriting row goes first up then down. Before starting the campaign person has high level of confidence may be in over form but as time passes, that level becomes down accordingly. Actually, this is peak navigational outputs of some fundamental personality traits, in which condition person becomes highly active or reactive to a certain extent. During that stage, person does not have correlation with his circumstances and condition, having full lack of intelligence. This is the "reverse action of lowest form of confidence". The symptom in observed in handwriting as the alignment of handwriting gets started towards upside then goes downward. The phenomenon would be observed is many segments in a single row of handwriting.

(iv)   Logic power in depressed person is observed abnormally very strong but it is quite difficult to express those practically on correlation with general circumstances and factors. Nevertheless, person could not mend his emotional system, even though he knows his logics ore not relevant. In handwriting, it is reflected as that the letters of some words one are abnormally is dislocated at some places. Indeed, the depressive mood system strongly looks for his supportive factors to be actively sustained. In connection of this symptom some letter are abnormally wider, through which it is revealed the searching of supporting factors by the abnormal depressive mood system.

(v)   In handwriting sample of depressed person, among some words there are more spacing that is abnormal are observed in unnatural fashion. The abnormality observed as first row of handwriting commonly shows normal spacing. The symptoms reveal mental disownity. Generally depressed person looks for escaping way away from his depression causing circumstances and factors.

In bilingual (English & other language) person with his mother language, show abnormal spacing everywhere in handwriting. No rhythm is observed in his mother language with abnormal spacing. Most of depressed person shows abnormal fast handwriting.

Writing with high speed and his signature prominently than that of handwriting sample reflects the high speed.

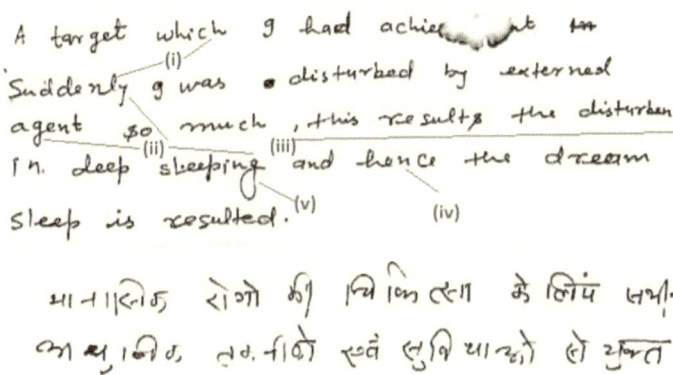

Fig. 1.2

Description of depression – Depression will be diagnosed as -

Cluster of hanging letters + g loop + fluctuated row + abnormally isolated letters + abnormal spacing.

A.   Important Traits To Be Considered Accordingly While Making Report -

Towards reforming personality traits through intrapersonal communication by neural pathways of those via brain learning, personality research report is required as mentioned earlier and to prepare therapeutic personality research report consist of all instructions to be communicated and "state of mind" along. There are following important traits to be considered according to the unique personality revealed by handwriting sample for communication, consulting guidance or counseling towards empowering personality traits would lead to mental empowerment with cure. Well, considering these all are not mandatory and strictly depend on what handwriting reveals, which may let permit to add new traits not mentioned here. The traits are characterized here by as handwriting depicted by chronic psychopaths. On missing any or many characteristics, change in guidance format will occur accordingly. Well during preparation of therapeutic personality research report, these following suggestions should be kept in mind. If person is on self-cure, he must prepare his therapeutic research report this way towards curing. Because of being unique personality, report will be unique so, uniqueness must be kept under deep consideration and differences should be identified according to form, presence and absence of characteristics –

1. On any matter confidence of person remains earlier high, then slowly down. Therefore for the person it would not be better to plan hardly before working or self presentation and at the same time he should not give it more importance because of having such person has condition based confidence instead of self based. This is depicted in handwriting as -

    (i)   Fluctuation occurred in baseline as that goes up then down.
    (ii) Commonly bigger loop is observed in lower zone.

2. Such person must not be hard logical on every point in normal behavior because of being high possibilities of getting person stucked on particular matter. Handwriting reveals this trait as –

    (i)   Signature done with slow speed
    (ii) Irregular gap among two successive words.
    (iii) Rare occurrence of uphill slants.

3. Keeping self safe from the circumstances unnecessarily would not be better and person should not do any sort of efforts regarding this concern no one is against him because it is very necessary to run normal procedures of general affairs in the mind as such people have person and condition born fear revealed in handwriting as –

    (i)   Abnormality observed in s loop as somewhere it is seen and somewhere not.
    (ii) Vibration observed handwriting

(iii) In handwriting sample there are specific and unnecessary deformations.

4. Being straightforward is necessary for the person because of such people have bigger problem in expressing themselves. This is revealed in handwriting as –

(i) Lack of rhythm occurs in handwriting.
(ii) Lack of similarities in same alphabets in whole handwriting.

5. Person should take help of as rational assistance from experts who are closed to create new ideas and thought as person has deep of need of mental expansion in greater context of new thoughts and idea. The trait reveled by handwriting as –

(i) Handwriting and signature both are not upward going.
(ii) Irregular pressure on the paper while writing.
(iii) More circular folds are observed than acute folds.
(iv) Most of letters are almost same.

6. Being obstinate regarding working which is subject born rather than behavior would be more beneficial because condition born obstinacy is more prominent in such person as handwriting reveals by –

(i) Handwriting goes upwards first then downward.
(ii) Some letters are observed in hanging form
(iii) In handwriting starched letters are prominently observed.

7. Person should note down all new ideas come in mind and correlate with facts of normal and routine practice because insufficient options and improper rational process are common occurrence in such people revealed in handwriting as –

(i) There are much more circular folds in handwriting sample
(ii) Speed of handwriting is more than normal.
(iii) Irregular gap among between two successive words.

8. Imagination of pleasure about coming condition and circumstances play very important role in curing as making most of things according to person's personality. Person must avoid imaging danger this is depicted by handwriting as –

   (i) Disturbed rhythm of handwriting that breaks flow of handwriting.
   (ii) Many letters are observed as breaking agent like – y, d, t and n.
   (iii) S letter is observed more decorated in additional form.
   (iv) The irregular gap observed in handwriting sample.

9. Conceding hardship about would not be better for the person because this trait is more dominating in such people as which is characterized in handwriting as –

   (i) Unusual deformations are observed in handwriting.
   (ii) More overwriting observed in handwriting.
   (iii) Breaking shields may be observed in signature.

10. Using anything for longtime does not affect person appropriately, therefore after certain time period there must be effective change in procedure of using because such people use most of things regarding use which is depicted by handwriting as –

    (i) Unlike handwriting sample some letters of sample are observed in erected form.
    (ii) Signature observed in upward going.
    (iii) Letters are observed in complete form.
    (iv) Speed of handwriting observed more than normal.

11. Reviewing work done again and again by the person will not be healthy on mental level, this is not advisable as such people has more negative attitude which is depicted by handwriting as –

    (i) Very big "g" loop observed in handwriting.
    (ii) Fluctuation in alignment of handwriting sample.

(iii)   Pressure observed from upside in handwriting sample.

(iv)   Placement of letter observed not in proper fashion.

12. Using more patience for such people is not so good therefore it must be time bounded as such people use this trait or bound to use. This is depicted by handwriting as –

(i)   Underlined signature.

(ii)   Regular deformation observed in whole handwriting sample.

(iii)   Some letters of handwriting sample observed very bigger in size.

(iv)   Letters observed in complete form.

13. Such people must not keep gap of more than 15 minutes between two successive conditions as do not have concrete decision about coming condition and person has problem of condition born mental disownity along. this revealed in handwriting as –

(i)   Very much gap between two successive words observed in handwriting sample.

14. Such person should keep high speed of his development of campaign but under control, because confidence of person depends on output as result. This is revealed in handwriting as –

(i)   Accessories of relevant letters ended suddenly and not exceeded normally.

15. For the depressed person humbleness is very necessary for him because person must have to keep maximum opportunities to think and do positive. In such people there is huge lack of this type of opportunities, therefore such person must has to run his mentality on subjects provided or obtained from others, the trait is revealed in handwriting as –

(i)   Acute folds observed on unnecessary places of handwriting.

(ii)   All letters are closed.

(iii)   Signature has specific deformation.

16. The depressed person should get opportunities from rational exchange because preparation of ground for emotional attachment is necessary for the person. This is depicted by handwriting as –

   (i)   Letters of signature are not properly elevated.
   (ii) Middle part of signature does not have any sort of specification.

17. It is very good for depressed person to participate festivals, social functions and carnivals because of making strong sociality as depressed person has weak form of sociality. This is depicted by handwriting as –

   (i)   Complete processing of words is not observed in handwriting.
   (ii)   Non manic form of handwriting.
   (iii) Single segmented signature.

A. **Graphotherapy** – On finding above-mentioned properties in a handwriting sample, following graphotherapies should be given. There is a point of mind that depression is not as chronic as dysthymic disorder i.e. person should have been suffering for not more than two years. These are the graphotharepies to be given as per requirement –

   (i)   In such person the depressive system becomes much strong and in gradual increasing form. All the depressed person have high and strong ambition and whenever it sounds him that could not be achieved with no factor is considered as a supporting factor towards achieving that ambition. It is a matter of hap chance in many of conditional factors that any of them is seemed as supporting in little bit, his confidence becomes up for short time period and there after it becomes down. There are two graphotharepies to make it normal -

   a.   Person should write straight lines with slow speed for five minutes and 2-5 times a day.

Fig. 1.2.i.a

It should one's keep eye on that gap between two lines should be in homogeneous form while drawing slanted lines. Drawing must not be in hurry.

It works on considering procedure of the factors in general form regarding normal activeness. The perception procedure of depressed person concerning his confidence is found in its specific form, which is just conditional. Being it in even a little bit of favorable, confidence gets abnormally strong and on being even little bit of unfavorable, drastically it gets down that is common in all depressed persons. Most of conditions around him are unfavorable. The graphotherapy stimulate the depressed person for homogeneous extension of activeness all type of condition.

b. For this trait another graphotherapy have to include creating new courses by intelligence for analyzing the condition for better perception.

Fig 1.2.i.b

This is 'V' with circular fold. All have to be practiced only for 2-5 minutes 5-10 times a day.

(ii) Such persons have strong logic power towards depressive system. The handwriting shows broken rhythm of mental flow which results formation of 'isolated letter' in words.

To maintain the mental flow through rhythm of logic power on various conditional factors, it is necessary to combine letters in rhythmic form.

Such letters have to be got into the habit of writing of the depressed person.

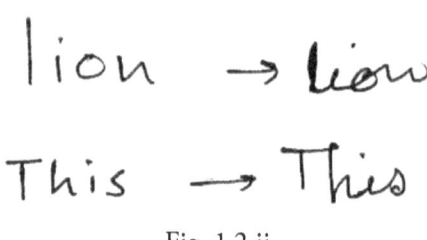

Fig. 1.2.ii

(iii) Hard obstinacy regarding achieving particular goal or ambition with creating concept of living plays important and significant role in depressed person. Hard obstinacy based personality makes person easy to percept according to his own ethos, indeed the depressed person look for other side in addition to getting not succeeded using conditional factors and circumstances properly due to losing his command on his summing depression causing circumstances, situations and conditional factors. Rather depressed person does not have proper obstinacy. To improve it person has to practice following doodle as graphotherapy -

Acute folds must be in this doodle, which have to be practiced 5-10 times for 2-5 minutes a day.

At the same time, depressed person have not to hide his obstinacy at any condition that must be expressed in any form. In addition to using obstinacy, the depressed person must have to be selective about his working.

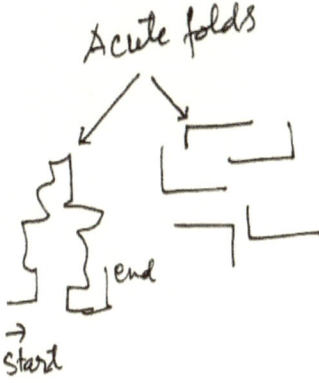

Fig. 1.2.iii

(iv) Rational assistance creates proper mode of perception having new courses, which is much more helpful in clearing ambition, being straightforward, opportunities to create new ideas, and thought and in addition to rational assistance has also strong potential to deviate the mind of depressed persons towards new direction from depression causing factors. For such person it is very necessary to insist him towards rational assistance because they don't have it in proper from. In handwriting no proper elevation in letters in observed. To make it strong, the person have to practice following doodle 2-5 minutes for 4-6 times a day

This should be in gradual increasing order of elevation.

With the graphotharapy, the depressed person have to note down that all new ideas which come in his mind on any subject and then resemble to them with normal practices and practical routine.

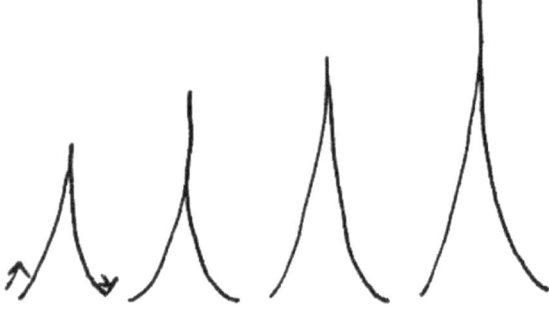

Fig. 1.2.iv

(v) As it is told that complete emotional mechanism based on four pillars, those are pleasure, danger, ego and sex. The depressed person has more chances of getting him feared. No condition or conditional factor makes him hopeful on any subject. Because of being disappointed from his normal running conditions wants to escape from that. The symptom reflects in handwriting as breaking of rhythmic flow of handwriting and breaking occurred in letters which are y, d, t and n and some letters are decorated additionally without regular gap.

There are three graphotherapies in this section -

(a) Depressed person must not decorate any letter additionally and space before or after must be lesser.

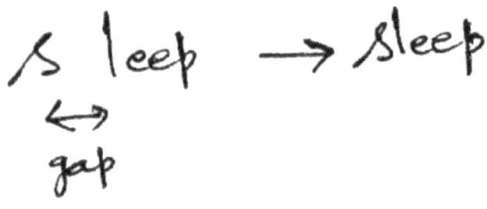

Fig. 1.2.v.a

(b) Letter must be written completely with their complete extension and uphill slants e.g.

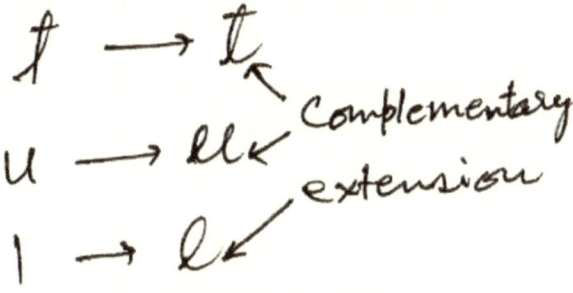

Fig. 1.2.v.b

(c) Commonly such letters are found somewhere in the handwriting not and regular way. Therefore, all letters must be regularizing as made on other places of handwriting.

(d) The last graphotharapy in this section is united or connected 'u' in upward going in upward direction with high speed.

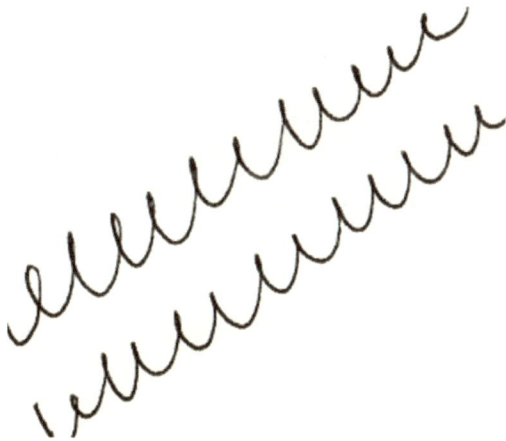

Fig. 1.2.v.d

This should be practiced 2-5 minutes 5-10 times a day.

(vi) It is necessary for person who is suffering from depression must not concede hardship about any concern because it directly damages natural way of life determined by rhythm of flow of logic power, which makes and maintains way of perception. In depressed person this deciphered reflects in handwriting as overwriting at somewhere and in signature as making shield. To get freed from such hardship conceding abnormal trait, there are following graphotherepies-

(a) Person must avoid over writing and
(b) Avoid making shields and stylish shapes in handwriting. Instead of stylish signature he must sign as full name signature.

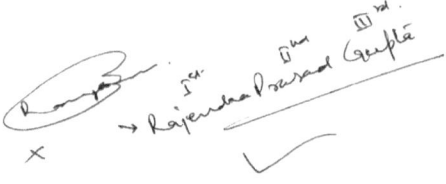

Fig. 1.2.vi.b

(vii) The depressed person must not review his work done again and again because it would lead gradual increment in negative attitude and pessimism as whole regarding almost concerns. The symptoms reflects in handwriting as 'g' 'y' 'j' having bigger lower loop which depicts severe pessimism in the person.

There are two graphotharapies

(a) g – loop must be lesser

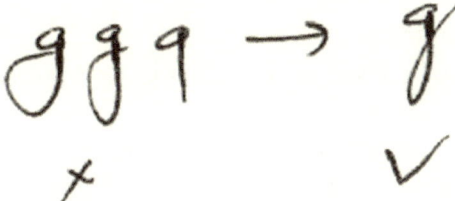

Fig. 1.2.vii.a

(b) I–w with connection should be practiced with triple underline. This should be done 2-5 minutes and 5 -10 times a day. Practice has to be done with high speed and all three underlines must be in regularly forward. The connected both two bodies must be left slanted.

Fig. 1.2.vi.b

(viii) The depressed person must not use more patience. After critical stage using more patience leads depression to increasing form gradually with the help of wanted or unwanted conditional factors. On the other hand, we can say that the procedure of using patience causes depression. It may be panic on more use. The critical stage of using patience for depressed person is defined as "stage on which the substitute of particular objective get started to come across mind". This is a state just after the depressed person must be highly active on substitutes of objective.

There are two doodles as graphotharepy.

(a) This should be practiced with high speed 2-5 minutes 4-6times a day. It stands to make person active.

Fig. 1.2.viii.a

(b) For depressed person, it is necessary to determine another goal after finishing one as come in his mind instantly.

It should be practiced with slow speed in starting then speed should be increased gradually with going to the top must not come down. The practiced schedule should be 2-5 minutes for 4-6 times a day.

Fig. 1.2.viii.b

(ix) The mental disowinity (the phenomenon in which many unwanted conditional factors and unnecessary new objective(s) beside his main goal become active due to more gap (more than of 15 minutes) between two successive conditions.) which is depicted in handwriting as more space among two words. The average space among two words as much as length of capital letter.

If the depressed person has such abnormality, as a graphotherapy he must bring improvements in the space to overcome his mental disownity.

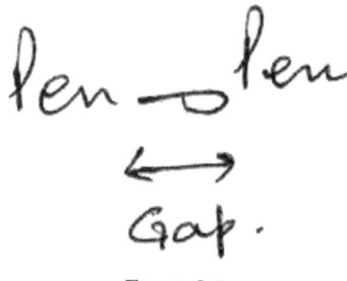

Fig. 1.2.ix

(x)   Person suffering from depression must have high speed of his development of working pattern. On being that slow, it results improper running of all traits regarding particular campaign. In handwriting it is depicted as some letters have sudden endings and not exceeded normally.

For this anomaly the following graphotherapy will be most useful-

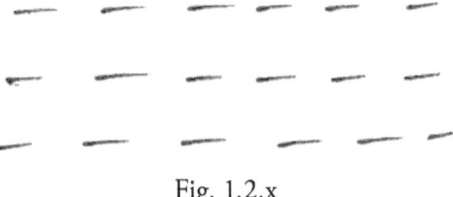

Fig. 1.2.x

It must be practiced with high speed for 2-5 minutes and 5-10 times daily.

(xi) **Drastic downfall in activeness of trait of sociality is observed in depressed person. He likes loneliness and do not want to attend new people rich condition, entertain people, guests, Festivals and other social functions. The unsociability of the person depicted in handwriting as lack of inverted 'c' and single unite of signature.**

To improve the sociality there are two graphotherapies-

(a) Signature should be two or more two or more than two segmented.

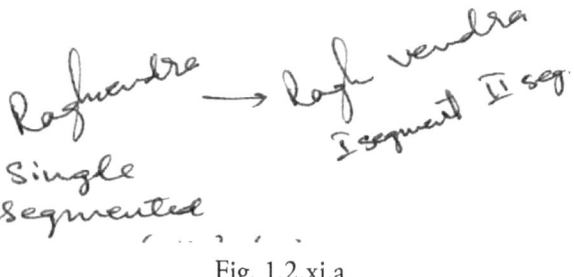

Fig. 1.2.xi.a

(b)

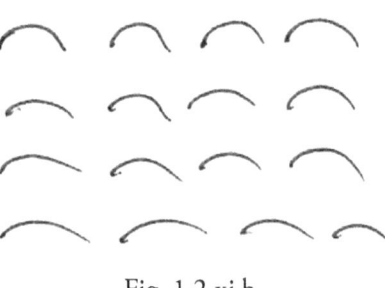

Fig. 1.2.xi.b

It should be practiced with slow speed for 2-5 minutes 5-10 times a day.

CHAPTER – 3

Bipolar Disorder

Bipolar disorder is also known as "manic depression" disorder", "manic-depressive disorder" or "bipolar affective". This is a mental illness classified into mood disorder by DSM (IV). Person with bipolar disorder experiences episodes of agitated mood known as mania and hypomania, depending on the severity alternating with episodes of depression.

There may be different levels of "mania" according to their severity may occur with different levels. At milder levels of mania, individuals appear energetic, excitable and may be highly productive. As mania becomes more severe, individuals begin to behave erratically and impulsively, often making poor decisions due to unrealistic ideas about the future, and may have great difficulty with sleep. At the most severe level, individuals can experience much distorted beliefs about the world known as psychosis.

Individuals who experiences manic episodes also commonly experience depressive episodes some experiences are mixed state in which symptoms of both mania and depression are involved. At the same time, manic and depressive episodes have been last for a few days to several months. According to data of Center for family guidance, Vergenia "about 4% of people suffer from bipolar disorder. Prevalence is similar in men and women and, broadly, across different cultures and ethnic groups. Genetic factors contribute substantially to the likelihood of developing bipolar disorder, and environmental factors are also implicated. Bipolar disorder is often treated with mood stabilizing medications and psychotherapy. In serious cases, in which there is a risk of harm to oneself or others, involuntary commitment may be used. These cases generally involve severe manic episodes with dangerous behavior or depressive episodes with suicidal ideation. There are widespread problems with social stigma, stereotypes, and prejudice against individuals with a diagnosis of bipolar".

As in this disorder, the person becomes feels manic and depression come frequently. This is why this also callcad "manic – depressive disorder ". There out three types of this disorder as explained in DSM IV

(i) Cyclothymic disorder – it is persistent chronic state of mood disturbance inpatient found in mood of person in which the behavior become depressive and hypomania both. Nevertheless, both do not have such survivors not to touch the criteria of DSM IV.

(ii) Bipolar I disorder – The person with this disorder has felt one or more than one depressive and manic episode.

(iii) Bipolar II disorder – In this category the person attests one hypomanic stage and more than one depressed mortal stage he has felt. During that experience, the mood of person become fluctuated in little bit of time but the sad conduct remain unaffected.

SYMPTOMS IN HANDWRITING – It is quite difficult to identify the differences among exactly the Bipolar I, Bipolar II and cyclothymic disorder through handwriting because of being much variable. Well on following symptoms it becomes some easy to diagnose. So, if following features are observed in handwriting there would be bipolar disorder-

(i) Person of bipolar disorder has right slanted handwriting because of manic mental form in which very least signs of depression in letters are observed. Most of mentalities are using personality traits are used in managing the manic form to feel euphoria.

(ii) Very big loops formed in g, j, z, and y rather than thin and bigger or single down stroke. The symptom reveals the presence of high negative thinking as well as negative attitudes about circumstances and situations as well including subjects. Such negative attitude causes person depression.

(iii) At somewhere in handwriting, some letters have blunt ends like d, f, t. In d blunt ends are seen regularly where as in t is observed quite irregular due to intermittent irritation and violation.

Diagnosis of Bipolar Disorder through Handwriting - Right slanted handwriting + t, d, f, are with blunt ends + very big loops formed in g, y, & z or single long down stroke.

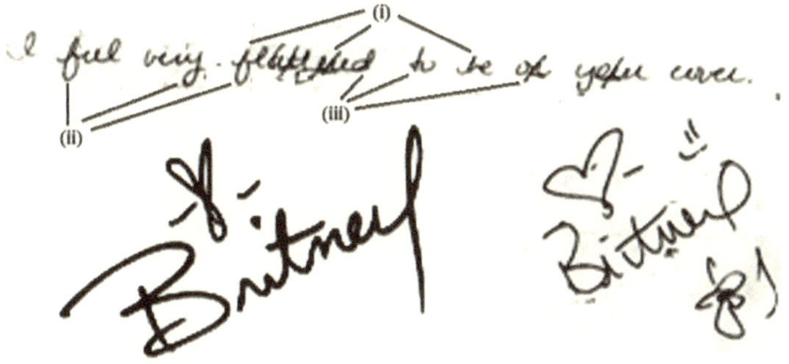

https://en.wikipedia.org/wiki/Britney_Spears#/
media/File:Britneyspearssignature.png

Fig. 1.3.1.

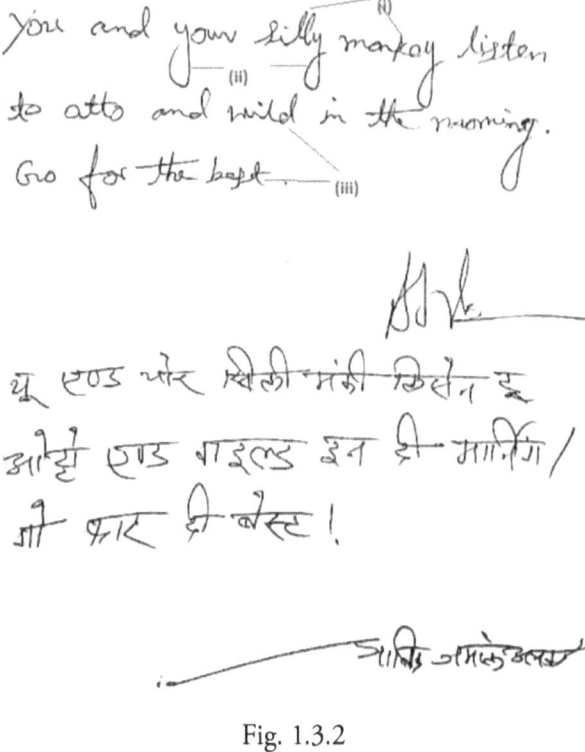

Fig. 1.3.2

B. Important Traits To Be Considered Accordingly While Making Report -

Towards reforming personality traits through intrapersonal communication by neural pathways of those via brain learning, personality research report is required as mentioned earlier and to prepare therapeutic personality research report consist of all instructions to be communicated and state of mind along. There are following important traits to be considered according to the unique personality revealed by handwriting sample for communication, consulting guidance or counseling towards empowering personality traits would lead to mental empowerment with cure. Well, considering these all are not mandatory and strictly depend upon what handwriting reveals, which may let permit to add new traits not mentioned here. The traits are characterized here by as handwriting depicted by chronic psychopaths. On missing any or many characteristics, change in guidance format will occur accordingly. Well during preparation of therapeutic personality research report, these following suggestions should be kept in mind. If person is on self-cure, he must prepare his therapeutic research report this way towards curing. Because of being unique personality, report will be unique so, uniqueness must be kept under deep consideration and differences should be identified according to form, presence and absence of characteristics –

Manic Portion –

1. Avoidance of considering tough tasks is necessary for bipolar person except very little bit of exception. Because confidence of person observed in negative form which is depicted by handwriting by –

    (i) Both handwriting and signature are downward going.
    (ii) Speed of handwriting is less than normal.
    (iii) More circular folds are observed in Hindi sample in comparison to English sample.
    (iv) Letters of words are not in complete form.
    (v) More pressure of pen imposed on paper at some places.

2. Bipolar person should avoid using more logical mind all time because of being more violent and using logic more logic power would make this more panic. This is revealed in handwriting as –

    (i) Speed of handwriting less than normal.
    (ii) Signature of person is observed commonly underlined.
    (iii) Regular gap among words.
    (iv) No uphill slant is observed in handwriting.

3. Positive review of work done may be necessary for bipolar person because such people always suppose themselves inferior to others depicted in handwriting as –

    (i) No complete circle is made in upper part of relevant letters either in English or Hindi sample.

(ii) Partially made circles and that does not cover own letter completely.

(iii) Letters are not in homogeneous form.

4. Blind obeying or following any one should be avoided and if person has any type of objection he must put it before strongly. Because person does not have strong concept about following or obeying. The trait is revealed in handwriting as –

(i) Hindi sample has elevated letters (as accessories) whereas English sample not.

(ii) Speed of handwriting less than normal.

(iii) Lack of bigger first letter in signature.

5. Bipolar person should have strong from of ego. Because of lacking healthy ego in bipolar person there is problem of self-identity in him therefore all matter subjected to this concern are in negative form. The trait is depicted by handwriting as –

(i) No big first letter in signature.

(ii) Low area covered by signature.

(iii) Handwriting is downward going.

(iv) Slow speed of handwriting.

(v) Signature is underlined.

6. Thinking of new thoughts whenever they come in the mind of bipolar person, should be consider seriously having concerns of their utilization and importance as bipolar person does not have concept of using things properly therefore no impact of proper use of things is observed. This is revealed in handwriting as –

(i) Letters are not properly elongated.

(ii) Signature is not upward going.

(iii) Letters are not complete.

(iv) Slow speed of handwriting.

(v) Many deformed letters are observed in handwriting.

7. For the bipolar person the making plans should be based on own thoughts and according to priorities because of having not superiority feeling that results person does not dominate the conditions. The trait revealed by handwriting as –

   (i)   There is no loop observed in upper part of relevant letters.
   (ii) The shape of letter is not observed in homogeneous form.

8. Bipolar person should enjoy all conditions and situations in different way because person has homogeneous extension of factors of typed pleasure with many factors of danger the trait is depicted by handwriting as –

   (i)   Homogeneous flow in handwriting.
   (ii) There are many sudden ends or breaks in handwriting.
   (iii) There is no decoration in letters at all.
   (iv) No regular gap among words.

9. It's very necessary to conclude the campaign, works or projects for the bipolar person because there is lack of concluding trait in personality which is revealed by handwriting as –

   (i)   All deformities in letters of handwriting have homogeneous format.

10. Bipolar person should determine his effective role in all conditions because there is very poor form of trait of determination in such people which is depicted by handwriting as –

    (i)   First letter is not bigger.
    (ii) Uphill slants are not in proper number.
    (iii) Lack of accessories in the signature.
    (iv) Improper or lack mark in signature.

11. Punctuality is very necessary for bipolar person because of not having punctual routine of working, the trait is depicted by handwriting as –

   (i)   Though the needle point n hump is present but no extension observed in handwriting.
   (ii) Not bigger area covered by capital letters "A" and other relevant letters.
   (iii) No significant loop is observed in letter "h", "d" and relevant letters.

12. All reason of subjected to violation and fond should be clear to the bipolar person because of having many reasons of violation which is depicted by handwriting as -

(i)   Presence blunt end "t", l, d-stem and other letters having blunt end.

13. Bipolar person should be introvert because of being them highly extrovert that is why internally no system could take place in them. The trait is depicted by –

   (i)   There are many open letters observed in handwriting.
   (ii) Some letters are in compressed form.
   (iii) There may abnormal creations observed inside the relevant letters.

14. Bipolar person should use things completely because it is very necessary to have complete impact of processes of using things as person does not use things properly, depicted in handwriting as –

   (i)   Letters are inappropriately elongated and elevated.
   (ii) Abnormally some letters are not completed.
   (iii) Slow speed of handwriting.
   (iv) There is some sort of deformation observed as a part of letters.

15. Bipolar person should not be in hurry or in hasten because of being abnormal high impact of condition and their factors due to having more sensitivity towards it that results person is not normal about it. The is revealed in handwriting as –

    (i)   More fluctuation observed in speed of handwriting.
    (ii)   No outgrowth observed in the end of signature.
    (iii)   No careful formation of letters.

16. Bipolar person should have his own natural ideal to get inspired as he wants to be in future as person does not have such type of this concept. This is reflected in handwriting as –

    (i)   In signature no upper zone stroke is observed.
    (ii)   No abnormal change is observed in handwriting.

17. There should be strong obstinacy about the condition in bipolar person because of being person born obstinacy directly affects the behavior in negative way. The trait is depicted as –

    (i)   Smaller shape of letters.
    (ii)   Smaller signature.
    (iii)   Normally signature goes in straight line.
    (iv)   Words are not well furnished.

18. Bipolar person should pay his intension about using artistry (music, sketching, painting, drawing, writing) or creative works as in such person there is trait of artistry in them but they do not use properly. Therefore, to expand the mental scope this would be quiet better. This is revealed in handwriting as-

    (i)   Slight manic form of handwriting.
    (ii)   Slow speed of handwriting.
    (iii)   At some places there is more pressure imposed by pen on the paper.

B. Grahpotherapies – To cure this abnormality there are following doodles should be use as graphotherapy.

(i)   Proper feeling of responsibility keep person on right way by providing contemporary goals. Therefore, proper responsibilities in with proper strength keep person away from worthless emotional fluctuation. The responsibility feelings in person of bipolar disorder person are not in proper form. According to requirements of current time, the person depends on conditions, which are the major cause of being mal adoption, the lack of responsibility feeling raveled in handwriting as absence of loop in lower case letter of "s" or shown in figure below. To improve or reform the responsibility feeling in bipolar disorder there is following doodle should be as a graphotherahy.

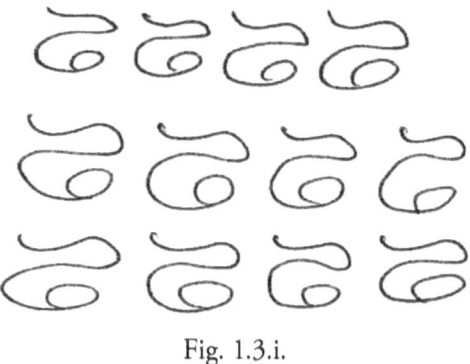

Fig. 1.3.i.

It should be practiced with slow speed for 2-5minuts 4-6 times a day.

(ii)   Bipolar personality disorder suffering person has poor form of trait of logic power and because of that they have much difficulties to analyze the events and topics, circumstances etc. and just due to this disability, they cannot have proper reasonable cause about any happenings. If conclusion goes in favor of person, that would cause mania and whereas if that is unfavorable to the person would cause depression.

Therefore, it is necessary to make strong the logic power. To do this person has to draw just vertical standing lines on white paper. This is responsible to find the exact logically justified position of person in any conditions and salutations. It should be preceded with normal speed and length must not be less than 1.5 cm. The duration of practicing 2-5 minutes and 4-6 times a day.

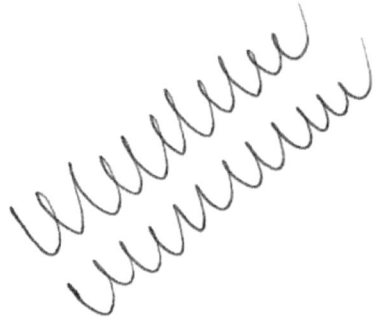

Fig. 1.3.ii

(iii) Such person should have to determine their conditional status logically. However, signature of such person reveals high ambition with least fluctuation. The letters are observed having slight changes in t or deformed with some extra out growth, additional deformation style of writing as they should be written or with both. Therefore following doodle should be prescribed to the person towards clearing his ambition.

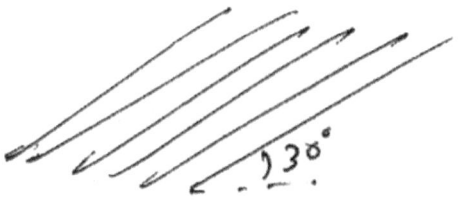

Fig. 1.3.iii

There are slanted lines should be practiced by person for 5 to10 a day times for 2 to 5 minutes. The angle of slant should be between 30 and 45⁰. The speed of practicing should be prescribed high to such person towards clearing their ambition.

(iv) Bipolar disorder suffering person has strong negative attitude causes depression to the person. This is because of over valuation of their work and results repeatedly. If those of them are in feasible the person become manic and while infeasible the person become depressed, the negative altitude is revealed in handwriting as very big loop formed in g, j and z therefore to rid person off such negative attitudes there is following graphotherapy –

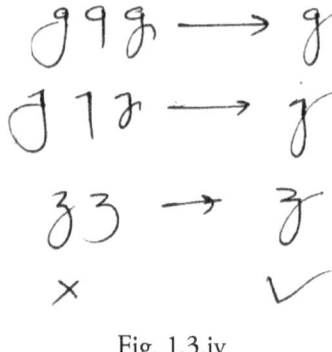

Fig. 1.3.iv

Loop must be thin, long and tail must crossing body

(v) Such person does not have proper intelligence and happiness come in intermittent form across mind. The lack of intelligence is revealed by handwriting as lacking of uphill slants. To vanquish the abnormality the person must have to be freed the past. There is a following doodle as a grtaphotherapy-

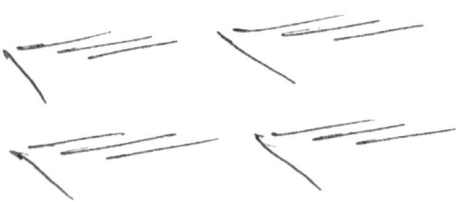

Fig. 1.3.v

There is a two parts of this doodle one left in slanted line (I) and three flag lines, Flag lines must be upraised going, It should be provided to practice to the person for 2.5 minutes and 4-6 times a day.

(vi) In the handwriting of such persons, it is often observed that t- bar is not observed in homogeneous and regular fashion. The phenomenon reveals the fact 'that enthusiasm of person is in fluctuating form" cusses person abnormal sensitivity about their circumstances and situation. Sometimes it makes person stacked to the situation and sometimes being insensitive, this emotional phenomenon directly affects the presentation of the person.

It is quite necessary to make enthusiasm in homogenous and consistent form. The following change in handwriting is the most suitable for this. The person always must place 't' bar quite move than half of its height.

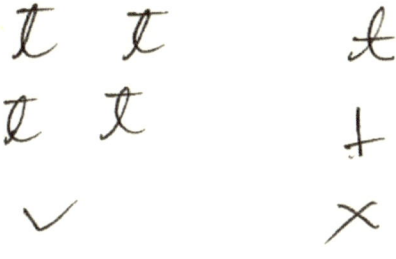

Fig. 1.3.vi

Depressive disorder will treated as described earlier according to personality depicted by unique handwriting.

UNIT - 2

ANXIETY DISORDER

According to DSM (IV) the anxiety disorder is referred as the person feels unreal anxiety and irrational fear in such amount that his normal life becomes maladapted as well as clearly anxiety is expressed. These are six types of anxiety disorder according to DSM-IV

1- Phobia
2- Panic disorder
3- Generalized Anxiety Disorder GAD.
4- Obsessive compulsive disorder OCD.
5- Post trauma stresses disorder PTSD.
6- Active stress disorder.

Out of above 6 mentioned disorders two of them are fear disorders i.e. Phobia and Post Traumatic Stress disorder because of concerning with various things or conditions where as rest of disorders are not. The reason behind this is due to not coming person to anxiety causing factors and conditions directly related to fear. Therefore, except these of two all four disorder are recommended to keep in anxiety disorder by Seligman & Roshechan (1998) defines Phobia as "Phobia is a continues fear which is quite beyond in proportion to realties."

Chapter – 1

Phobia

According to DSM (IV) the anxiety disorder is referred as the person feels unreal anxiety and irrational fear in such amount that his normal life becomes maladapted as well as clearly anxiety is expressed. Phobia is the most common anxiety disorder. Person has persistent form of fear in disproportionate form which is not dangerous in real and if then dangerous at zero extent. For example if a person has phobia with height then he will not go high despite being completely safe and on persisting this in person his conduct and behavior may become deviated.

Saligman and Rosenhan (1998) define phobias as "phobia is a continuous and persistent fear which is quite beyond proportion and realities".

Phobia suffering person is feared of such things or conditions, which are quite out of proportion and are not dangerous reality and because of this the conduct, behavior and general routine of life of person becomes maladapted. On this point phobia differs from general that because general fear maladapted form does not occurs.

Clinical symptoms of Phobias – There are following symptoms of phobias according to American Psychiatric Association (APA – 1994)-

a- Quite more fear than real proportion because of specific Condition or object.

b- On facing those fear causing object or condition, sever anxiety and panic attack occurs.

c- Person seems under persistent, sever and unreal fear.

d- He likes to be much more far from phobia causing objects or conditions.

e- If all above symptoms are not produced by other illnesses or causes.

In addition to this, other symptoms like headache, backache, and indigestion, stress etc. may be occurred in person. During panic attack, the person feels depersonalization and at the same time he also feels unreality with strange. Rather symptom of depression may also be observed. In some people, symptoms of interpersonal difficulties may be observed and some feels problems in taking decision, which is referred "decide phobia".

Symptoms depicted by Handwriting - In handwriting the phobia is revealed as-

(i) The elevation having letters like b, d, f, h, k, l, t, and all capital letters are   made with "abnormally high elevation" depicts over mental activities in phobia suffering person. In some cases, abnormal long strokes are also observed. He excessively thinks quite to justify all about that particular object on logical ground as he has. The mental process results many unwanted subject and condition born factors cause irrational fear in out of proportion. The high elevation of letters and long strokes depict the extra use to initiate the irrational imaginary power using contemporarily useless conditional factors about phobia in its greater context.

(ii) There are many deformed letters are observed in handwriting which may be in any form like in elevation, width, in down strokes, in outgrowths of letters etc. The reason behind deformation is due to giving unusual reaction on consideration of many unwanted and fearing objects or factors. After deformation in letters, there is no proper elevation in letters observed. Another feature is seen in phobic people who are bilingual (one is his mother language and other one is foreign language) that is "change in slants" as big anomaly clearly observed in "elevated letters". E.g., If English is right slanted and Hindi is left and vice-versa but it is not a significant feature.

(iii) Many letters show regular vibration. It is observed obviously in that person who has been suffering from phobia since 2 years due to any unwanted event, conditional factors or by any cause. However, in chronic phobia person vibration is reflected in regular in trace amount to be observed carefully. At the same time symptoms in chronic person also have tendency of fast writing and they become slow at some letters where and at that time vibration can be observed easily.

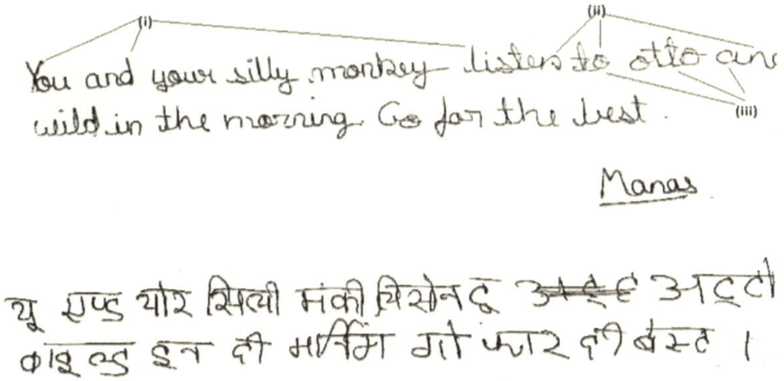

Fig. 2.1.1

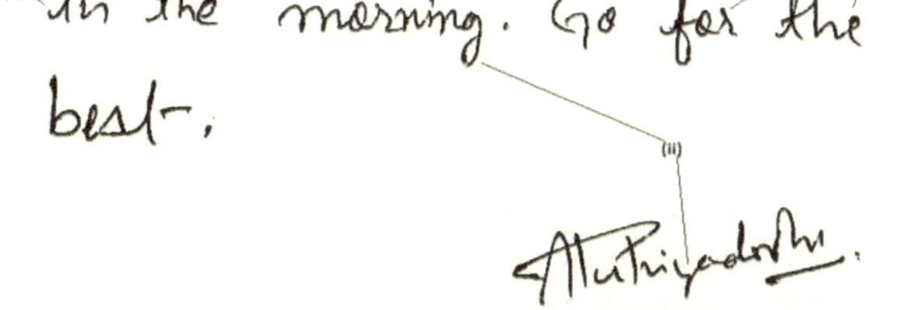

Fig. 2.1.2

A. **Peak Navigational Traits To Be Kept in Mind Accordingly While Making Report -**

Towards reforming personality traits through intrapersonal communication neural pathways of concerning traits via brain learning, personality research report is required as mentioned earlier and to prepare therapeutic personality research report. Unlike others in case of phobia, reaction of body comes out from mind in form of fear against particular object, which is result of correlation of "Peak Navigational Traits" with external stimulus. The phenomenon holds concept that in "to cause phobia there is no direct involvement of fundamental personality traits". This is the very reason that phobia does not harm personality but the problem then arises when body becomes reactive against any object and due to which psychosomatic attack occurs and person tries to keep abject away from him and conditions along. There are more than 100 types of phobias are diagnosed where as infinite number of phobias are still undiagnosed. That could be get through "Emotional Engineering" via understanding "Emotional Mechanism" as infinite number of external stimuli exist in circumstances when will any particular stimulus will come under correlation with "Peak Navigational Trait" depends upon that particular situation how cause of anxiety is being tackled with. Therefore, intrapersonal communication therapeutic personality research report must be made strictly on contemporary data revealed by handwriting. Reports of any two individuals may be throughout different. That is why all active personality traits are very important regarding diagnosis of peak navigational traits.

B. **Graphotherapies** – On finding these symptoms in handwriting sample, following graphotharepies are suitable for phobia person towards curing may be used as per requirement of personality –

(i) The phobic people are more sensitive about their unwanted events or happening related to phobia causing specific object. Therefore, they must have to pay more intention on their working and objective in greater context. They should have to keep a phrase in their mind that is "work done is more necessary than working". The symptom is observed in handwriting as occurrence of many acute folds in upper zone of letters and not decreasing in number with their blunt endings. In spite of having clear goal, person has unclear procedure towards achieving that. That is why it is necessary to make then dear the contemporary target or objective and goal and there after they have to make active on the process of achieving next goal of just after completing one. There are two graphotharepies regarding this concern –

(a) Make a circle and then draw a live just above that –

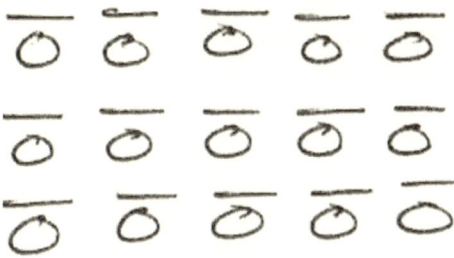

Fig. 2.1.i.a

It should be practiced with slows peed for 2-5 minutes 4-6 times a day.

(b) Next graphotharepy in this section is like z with more long tail than that of head. It should be practiced with high speed as above mentioned –

Head Tail

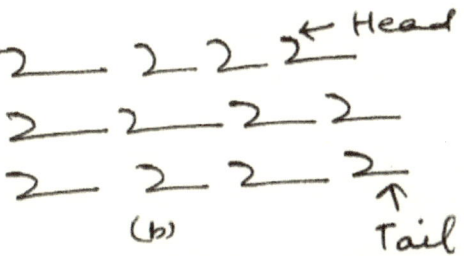

Fig. 2.1.i.b.

(ii) Normally phobic person does not look happy due to extra impact of in unwanted events and happenings. Happiness is relaxing form of person with positive & pleasant impact of conditional factors. In opposite to this fact if any person is happy having negative impact of condition factors caused by subject of phobia, the person should get the points of pleasure from current conditions according to his own personal liking. Therefore, it is necessary of being happiness to the person as an active trait.

The graphothorapy, which is helpful to do this with intelligence and keep this trait in full of its function, given below –

Fig. 2.1.ii

Must be upward going and must be practiced with high speed for 2 to 5 minutes 4-6 times a day at the same time.

(iii) Generally, phobic person has difficulties in maintaining the rhythm of presentation on various conditions, which are coming in sequence as per requirement of situations and conditional demand. Indeed the breaking of rhythm makes phobic person intending towards its causes have high possibilities to correlate with the cause of phobia. To keep away the person from such type of any possibility or causes of phobia, it is necessary that not being the break of rhythmic continuity of flow of conditions with various factors. Following graphotherepy will be most suitable to do this –

Person has to write combined lettered words with slow speed during stating starting and the gradually he should increase the speed of writing e.g.

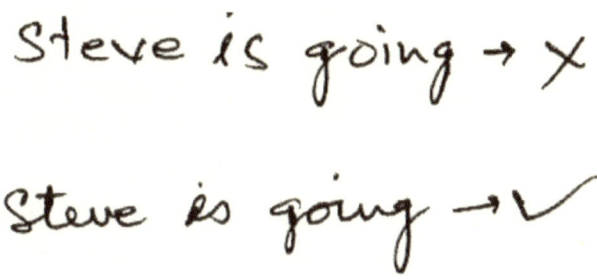

Fig. 2.1.iii

(iv) Phobic person has high mental activity. They use their mind quite more than those of normal people, which is reflected by in handwriting as high elevation having letters. The rhythmic break correlates herewith and that results break in "mental continuity." Following doodle as a graphotherapy stands to reform this abnormality.

It should be practiced with slow speed for 4-6 times and 2-5 minutes. Here a fact, that matters to be kept mind that the "elevation of doodle" and "gap between two units". The elevation of doodle must not be less than 2-5 cm and gap between two units should be 0.5 cm should not be exceeded from its limit. All units must be in about same size.

Fig. 2.1.iv.

(v)   Phobic person has least number of opportunities of considering more factor intelligently belongs either to their field or apart from of that. Such mental status makes phobic person rigid and create ground of keeping person away from rational form. Such person open himself which are quite privacy of phobia, is observed in them and taken as controversial form. In handwriting, the processes of closing the letters like a, o, and d has anomalies. To rid them off from this abnormal trait, they need to be more talkative considering more and more factors provided them passively by conversation. The following doodle for graphotharepy stands to make it in the way-

These are open circles from upper side these should be practiced with slow speed initial stage and then (i.e. after one weak to 10 days) the speed should be increased. The patter of practice is 2.5 minutes 4-6 times a day.

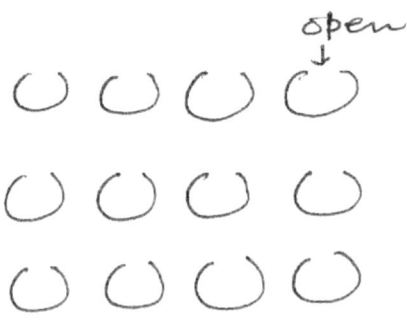

Fig. 2.1.v

(vi)   Lack of proper fondness observed in phobic persons due formation of rhythm of most liked tinny conditional factors could not take place properly. Formation of fond trait is necessary in phobic person. Additional fondness is quite helpful to provide him positive cause, vision and other liking views in phobia causing factors, which help in eradicating phobia and empowering his mind with willing of doing something for his founded person or fond causing factors. The activeness of doing something also includes phobia-causing factors. Gradually person starts learning how to deal with his phobia in positive way. To enhance fondness there is following doodle as a graphotherepy –

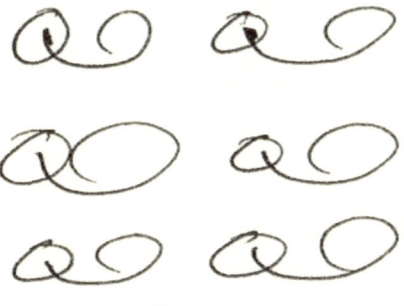

Fig. 2.1.vi

It should be practiced for 2-5 minutes for 5-10 for times a day with normal speed. Procedure of formation of doodle must keep in mind.

(vii)   The goal setting in such person creates abnormally more attraction towards it, which has least possibilities to correlate with normal phenomenon and contemporary conditional factors as well as person born factors. Such mental status results arising anxiety in form of phobia. Therefore, for the phobic person, it is necessary to clear his goal and the activities having proper possibilities to correlate with most of available conditions and factors in positive way. On proper correlation there are many possibilities are produced regarding thrive of persons. Possibilities even on thinking person become free from phobia causing factors. As their concerned compulsion that depends upon form of possibilities that how much attraction he has have towards goal.

To create such pathways there is following doodle as graphotherepy-

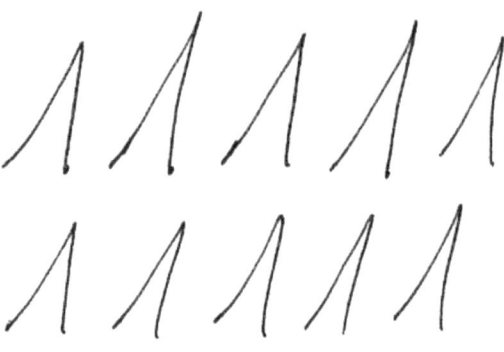

Fig. 2.1.vii

The graphotharepy stands for "utilizing present conditional factors with proper prospect." It should be minded here doodle is right slanted have to be practiced with normal speed for 4-6 times a day for 2-5 minutes.

(viii) Handwriting of phobic person shows abnormal spacing between two successive words that results arising of controversial form of mental activeness about coming conditions takes time between two successive conditions and if that is enough than normal results "Condition born mental disownity." The mental overlapping is caused due to lesser spacing among the words in which the person could not utilize his mental status fully regarding coming conditions. In other words we can also say person does not enjoy any condition completely. Any thought of any particular condition get shifted in next condition e.g. if a person has to go anywhere after taking bath & breakfast, on not giving proper time to particular tasks before tackling them mentality of bathing will run during breakfast and likewise this, that phenomenon will occur during going. This type of abnormality is depicted by handwriting as lesser spacing among words. The conditions born "mental disownity" because of occurring more gaps between two words. The phobia-suffering person with this abnormality has determined with contemporary specified target including many related conditions. Between any two successive conditions because of being more gap (more than 7 minutes) there may be many unwanted factor to come under person's consideration as substitute of that particular contemporary target. Those unwanted substitutes by which person becomes would easily deviate from his contemporary target. Such deviation after sometimes creates more anxiety may be as in greater problem of procrastination.

In phobic person both forms "the condition born mental overlapping" and "mental disownity" are observed. During initial stage of any campaign run by person, the mental overlapping is observed and later on due to more anxiety the mental disownity is also gets started. Both create anxiety. In handwriting, the start begins with lesser spacing is shown whereas ending with more spacing.

So, as a graphotherapy the phobia person have to mind his spacing during writing which must not be less than 0.5 cm and not more than 1.0 cm. It must be practiced carefully.

Fig. 2.1.viii

(ix) It is found that the phobic person has "endless concept of working" on any campaign or task. If that person is not working on any particular endless program or campaign then even that is very big problem for him in itself. The endless concepts create more anxiety because being mind always remains in search. The endless concepts depicted in handwriting as dissimilar the concluding letter, abnormal occurrence of vibration in whole handwriting. At the same time, the concluding form of letters is also not seen in handwriting.

To check the continuity of anxiety producing factors and causes there is a following doodle as a graphotharepy-
It should be practiced in little bit of higher speed than normal, which stands for making limits of concepts about campaigns or program. Little bit means maximum just up to 10 to 14 days.

Fig. 2.1.ix

It also has to same pattern of practicing that is 2-5 minutes for 4-6 times a day.

CHAPTER – 2

Panic Disorder

Panic disorder is a one of the most serious disorder of anxiety in which the person gets sudden attack of inexplicable panic attack. Such attacks repeat again & again or at least twice a week, referred as 'Panic attack' according to DSM-IV.

Panic attack is defined into 13 physiological sensations. When a person experiences any of 4 out of 13 symptoms, he would be categorized under 'panic disorder'. These 13 physiological sensations regarding this disorder are as follows-

1- Abnormal heart beat
2- Sweating
3- Muscular shivering
4- Feeling of retarded breathing or of being choked
5- Feeling of choking
6- Pain in stomach and vomiting
7- Chest ache
8- Unconsciousness or headache
9- Lack of realization or depersonalization
10- Feeling of losing self-control or becoming crazy
11- Fear of dying
12- Sensation of numbness or tingling
13- Sensation of much more hot or cold

Severe panic attack repeats at least twice a weak certainly. This would be cured but curing directly depends upon particular related conditions, stimulant and other external conditional factors. On facing those causes, the person is attacked of this disorder. It may start in early adulthood and directly related to stress creates enough more anxiety and experiences of stressful life. Sometimes panic attack is unexpected and comes suddenly or more frequently.

Symptoms in handwriting – The panic disorder is depicted by handwriting as-

(i) In whole handwriting, many deformed letters are seen because of negative impact of conditions and their factors. However, it would be some difficult task to see in general handwriting deformed complication as well as in signature. Normally person with panic disorder are more self-centered than normal person, which is revealed by handwriting with some exceptions. The self-centeredness is revealed by handwriting as being smaller size. Being a little bit more intellectual, more than normal, panic attack causing conditional factors are easily justified towards their strong negative impacts on personality of person. Therefore, least amount of similarity is observed in some same letters on observing whole handwriting sample.

(ii) Among words, there is more space among words cause condition born mental disowrity. There are strong possibilities of coming unwanted conditional factors under consideration of person liked by person later. Due to having strong attention on panic attack, most of conditional factors related to that abnormality come under deep consideration. This is deviation from his contemporary target or he is compelled to be deviated from his target. In this phenomenon, there is a strong possibility of getting him strong regarding use of mental security system. Being person self-centered, it would be the process to pay more intention to his outside circumstances having active security system. This is unnecessary activation of security system may lead to give harmful outputs. This is just like a started machine with no use.

(iii)   A very significant feature is observed in handwriting such abnormal person of panic attack that is "hanging accessories of letters". The phenomenon revealed in d, R, r, n, and u, the reason behind this is the "conflict to get away from the causes of panic attack as an unsuccessful task". This is difference between symptom of dysthymic and depression disorder in which whole word and one or two letters in a single word are seen in hanging form respectively the "hanging accessories of letters also show the "reluctance from some specific condition" that is contemporary goal which is also a one of the cause panic attack. It indicates the strong intention of person paid to such conditional factors.

(iv)   Other type of anomaly in such abnormal person is being higher t-bar in handwriting that means high enthusiasm in them having lowest possibilities of compromising with conditions. However, it would be a common in all persons who are suffering from abnormality of panic attack.

Panic disorder = Deformed letters + more space + hanging accessories of letters + High t-bar (may be or not)

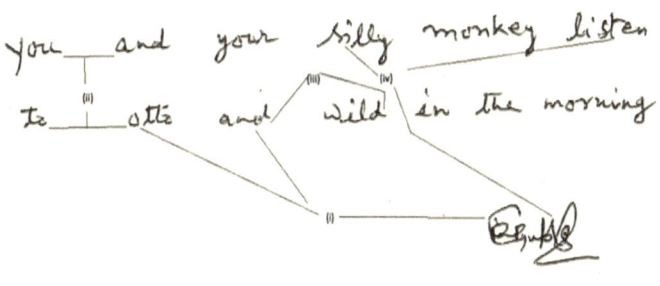

Fig. 2.2

B.   Important Traits To Be Considered Accordingly While Making Report -

Towards reforming personality traits through intrapersonal communication by neural pathways of those via brain learning, personality research report is required as mentioned earlier and to prepare therapeutic personality research report consist of all instructions to be communicated and state of mind along. There are following important traits to be considered according to the unique personality revealed by handwriting sample for communication, consulting guidance or counseling towards empowering personality traits would lead to mental empowerment with cure. Well, considering these all are not mandatory and strictly depend on what handwriting reveals, which may let permit to add new traits not mentioned here. The traits are characterized here by as handwriting depicted by chronic psychopaths. On missing any or many characteristics, change in guidance format will occur accordingly. Well during preparation of therapeutic personality research report, these following suggestions should be kept in mind. If person is on self-cure, he must prepare his therapeutic research report this way towards curing. Because of being unique personality, report will be unique so, uniqueness must be kept under deep consideration and differences should be identified according to form, presence and absence of characteristics –

1. For panic person consideration of highly emotional matters is not good. He should do his works using his mostly mind instead by heart. Because such people are highly emotional and due to which, he is deeply affected by such matters. The handwriting depicts this trait as –

   (i) There are much more differences occurred in accessories of letters.
   (ii) Words are intended to get connected with each other.
   (iii) Big loops are visible in many relevant letters in upper zone.

2. Such panic disorder person should take strong stand on logically hard ground because person already has strong logic power, depicted in handwriting as-

   (i) There is Normal speed of handwriting.
   (ii) There is upward going signature and handwriting.
   (iii) Signature is not underlined.
   (iv) Letters are abnormally isolated.

3. Person should correlate his ambition with normal realities because normal realities of person do not support the ambition of the person. This is revealed by handwriting as –

   (i) Signature is not underlined.
   (ii) No marking is in signature.
   (iii) Signature is completed with normal speed.
   (iv) In signature most of the letters look like touching base line.

4. Person suffering from panic disorder should avoid quick responding because such people are highly violent.

   (i) Handwriting has blunt end "t"
   (ii) Lower t bar.
   (iii) Loop is is formed in starting of signature.
   (iv) Signature is upward going which correlates with

5. There should not be created extra pressure of anything and to the some extent the panic disorder must be free from this pressure because conditional pressure as observed makes such person reactive depicted by handwriting as-

   (i) No uniformity is observed in letters with little bit of exceptions.
   (ii) More pressure due pen observed on the paper.
   (iii) No proper effort is observed in doing well furnishing the letters or words.

6. The panic disorder should pay attention towards using more artistry like music, arts and literature etc or other creative works because person is not provided the opportunities of raising his intellectual dimension revealed in handwriting as –

   (i) Slight manic form of handwriting.
   (ii) Abnormally more pressure imposed on paper due to pen.
   (iii) Abnormal speed of handwriting.

7. Between two different successive conditions there should be interval of 7 to 15 minutes in all condition because panic disorder person has both type of problems condition born mental overlapping due to lesser gap and condition born mental overlapping due to more gap. This is depicted by handwriting as –

    (i)   No homogeneousness is in gap between two successive words.

8. For panic disorder person should communicate on the basis of balanced extroversion and introversion because person has selective extroversion reflected in handwriting as –

    (i)   At somewhere "a" is open.
    (ii)   Some letters too compressed.
    (iii)   In "g" there is abnormal creation.

9. No doubt the attitude must be positive as such people do not have complete positive attitude. The trait is revealed by handwriting as-

    (i)   At somewhere "g" and "y" contains down stroke loops and somewhere not.
    (ii)   Slight fluctuation is observed in handwriting.
    (iii)   Signature is slight upward going.
    (iv)   There is inappropriate placement of letters.

10. Highly amusing reading material plays important role in improving penchant for reading because such people do not have proper amount of reading property depicted by handwriting as –

    (i)   Signature and handwriting sample both are not determined by base line.
    (ii)   Both signature and handwriting have definite rhythm.
    (iii)   Speed of handwriting is improper.
    (iv)   First letter of signature is made very big.

11. Complete imagination of fear causes is very necessary for the panic disorder person because person has conditional fear depicted in handwriting as –

    (i)   Vibration is observed in whole handwriting and signature.
    (ii)   Speed of writing is abnormally slow.
    (iii)   Abnormal deformations are observed in some letters.
    (iv)   Irregular alignment is in upward going handwriting.

12. Such people should avoid discussion with many people because of having both aggression and violation, revealed in handwriting as –

    (i)   Presence of blunt end 't'.
    (ii)   Many sudden endings are observed in handwriting.

13. Addressing group for such people will helpful in giving recognition on the self presentation as such people do not have better form of self – presentation, trait revealed in handwriting as –

    (i)   No shield is made in handwriting and signature.
    (ii)   Many out growths are observed in signature.

14. The panic disorder should not meet those people whom are not be liked by such person if this is necessary keep an assistant because though such people have good trait of meeting to the people but because of violation and emotional topsy-turvy, the impact may be negative. The good form of meeting trait is depicted by handwriting as –

(i)   Letters of the upper zone of signature make needle extension in 'k' and 'h'.
(ii)   Loop is formed in upper zone of letters 'h' and 'k'.
(iii)   Letters are not wider.

15. The panic disorder should give proper response on those thoughts, provided by any one because of bad form of trait of imitation in such person.

16. The panic disorder people should imagine him with view of other also the trait is characterized by handwriting as –

(i)   Only few letters are interconnected in signature.

(ii)   Differed down stroke is observed in single letter signature i.e. 'j'.

(iii) Irregular presences of acute and circular folds are in handwriting and signature both.

17. Imagination of pleasure in necessary for panic disorder person because person has feeling of danger revealed by handwriting as –

(i)   Many sudden breaks are observed in handwriting and signature.

(ii)   Some letters of handwriting are tried to decorate more but no overwriting at all.

(iii) No regular gap observed between two words in handwriting.

C. Graphotherapy - There are following graphotharepies to overcome the disorder of panic attack by reforming or creating new neural pathways of traits. It should be noted here that during attack graphotharepy does not work. Because of being apathic stage, person is unable to sense towards following the given instructions of graphotherapy. Grphotharepy works toward curing while there is least the possibility of attack to the person and being in all sense as well. Either there are following graphotherapies towards creating new neural pathways or reform, there are following graphotherapies -

(i)   Person suffering from panic disorder is observed as doing efforts to command the conditional circumstances to overcome the possibilities of panic attack. All time they have to keep continuous concern on every conditional factor, which would be dreadful to them along, they give serious look into most of all forms of situations. This is the reason of being formation of condition dependent confidence. The form of trait is interpreted in handwriting as fluctuation in alignment and many deformations in letters are frequently observed in handwriting sample. Instead of definite circular folds, many acute folds are observed while in other words acute folds replace circular folds. To have better control on conditions, the person must have to possess such form of confidence that does not get depended upon conditions and remain unaffected by circumstances as well. Confidences must be self-motivated. To make such of confidence to command the conditions and situation there is a following graphotharepy –

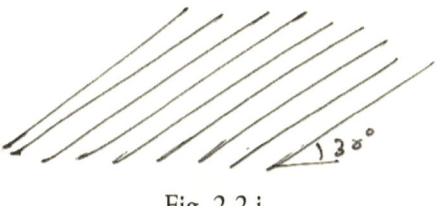

Fig. 2.2.i

The upward going slanted lines on 30-45⁰ on white paper for 2.5 minutes 5-10 times I days. This is responsible for clearing the form of "ambition". After clearance of attraction towards ambition makes his confidence self based. There after the person could have easy control on his conditions and circumstances. Having this practice, the person should change the form and look of his circumstances according to his own liking.

(ii) The person of panic disorder commonly has poor form of ego and proud results arising of many difficulties in formation of launching pad in society towards development. Because of being poor form of ego, he could not take decision firmly. Lack of affirmation is a common problem in panic disorder person. He could not take decision on their ego level. On the issue of ego he go easily to compromise that certainly should not be. The unhealthy ego is interpreted by panic disorder person as the first letter of handwriting not bigger, speed of handwriting is slow and signature does not cover more than normal area because of being not consideration of appropriate factors. Being healthy ego in panic disorder person, it is very necessary to cure with proper empowerment. To make healthy ego in such person, this graphotharepy is very useful which is very simple. The person should have to write bigger first letter. This should be a part of his regular practice.

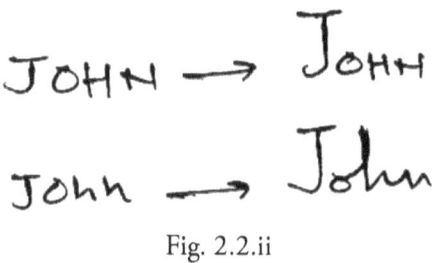

Fig. 2.2.ii

With practicing it as graphotharepy, he must bring it in his daily routine writing.

(iii) The person, who is suffering from panic disorder, does effort to find instant solution of problems. The stress which is result of procedure of getting solution or result instantly becomes cause of sever anxiety converts into panic attack. Normally it is found that they do not go to proper study the problem in systematic way. This entire phenomenon creates neural pathways of the weak trait of "solution seeking." The good form of this trait offers more strong studiousness in the person. The handwriting depicts "poor form of solution seeking trait" as no specific deformation is observed in handwriting. The fact reveals the good form of testing the subjects, which gets prolonged into good studiousness, signature covers normal area that means the person considers appropriate conditional factors related to his contemporary states and 'n' & 'm' humps are observed in handwriting.

Proper and active form of studiousness must be in panic disordered to cure. To reform or redevelop this trait there is following graphothorepy –

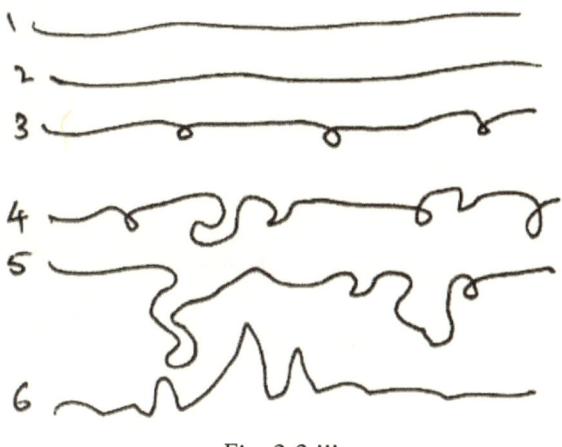

Fig. 2.2.iii

The upper two lines should be straight and then next should have deformation with some elevation. Size of deformation should be increased as coming down. It is noticeable here that the doodle should be practiced with very slow speed as much as he can for 2-5 minutes 5-10 times a day. It is not necessary to make deformations as shown in the figure. Only pattern following is important.

(iv) Panic disorder suffering person has strong and deep intention of looking past in specific concerns related to panic attack may be panic past. He also wants to repeat the preceding stage of panic attack with strong feeling of that If panic attack would have not be the situation would be quiet better. He thinks of his past as was quite better than present results strong affection with his past, which is interpreted by handwriting as some letters of handwriting are decorated unnecessarily with slow speed smaller size of handwriting and in signature is observed with back strokes. As on remedy such person should live lively in their present and must not compare their present with past. On comparing more, the possibilities of panic attack gets stronger. They should also use the available resources in new way and methods with clear prospect.

Therefore, it is necessary to make person free from above of memory, which are causing him panic disorder. To reform this trail, following trait should be practiced with high speed. There is two parts in this doodle one left slanted line (I) and three flag lines. Flag lines must be upward going. It should be practiced for 2-5 minutes and 5-10 times a day.

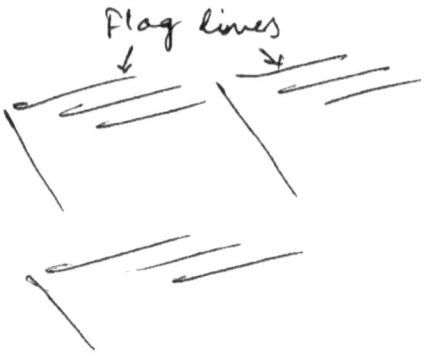

Fig. 2.2.iv

(v)   Happiness plays important role in curing panic disorder. It keeps person away from general stress causing factors and produces more interest in contemporary running and present conditions and their factors. The panic disordered person does not have or have very weak form trait of finding points of pleasure in a condition or situation. The trait of imagination does not support this trait. The phenomenon is depicted by handwriting by observation of some additional flow in handwriting which does not replaces the unwanted vibration, more gaps among two successive words caused by "mental disownity" due to which many unwanted conditional factors are permitted to be considered deeply and in handwriting. This depicted as one letter that covers whole letter causes many inauspicious and unwanted thoughts.

Panic disordered person must have strong trait to find out happiness and points of pleasure in all conditions according to own self. To created neural pathways concerning happiness and finding out that, there is following doodle as a graphotherapy –

Fig. 2.2.v

Elevation must not be less than 5cm. It should be practiced with high speed and upward going on 300 2-5 times and 5-10 times a day with high speed.

(vi) Person suffering from panic disorder does not have the trait of concluding the campaigns. End concluding trait plays significant role in providing proper satisfaction regarding campaigns. The endless campaign is one of the major and main causes of anxiety. Such person uses most of things related to campaign for long or endless time using all methods would be applicable. He does not utilize all rather systematically besides there is anyhow and random mode of utilization is applied without specification. Trait is depicted in handwriting as letters are not long and elevated because of not making or looking for concept to use the particular thing, letters are completed anyhow results occurring of many deformations on many places in handwriting sample. The phenomenon is due to conditional demand instead of it should be because of concept born and no letter is observed being deformation in outgrowths. The reason behind this is lacking of conditional prolongation on concept level and conceptual form trough out as well.

Panic disorder person must have the concluding concept to conclude their campaigns according to him or conditions. They must not use anything for long time. There should be change in place, in mode of using or that particular thing etc. and after certain time. To reform this trait easily there is following doodle as graphotharepy, which has to be practiced with high speed 2-5 minutes 4-6 times a day.

Fig. 2.2.vi

(vii) The panic disordered person feels many difficulties in expressing himself. The problem is just conditional with many unwanted conditional factors. On gradual prolonging such conditional phenomenon, person remains no longer to respect his own will. At the same time, he has to express himself forcibly and that is why he has to communicate properly with efforts rather than in natural way. Being his introvert, such person must be extrovert in overall behavior to tackle all the conditions all around. The introversion is reflected in handwriting as all letters are observed closed. No shield is seen in signature and English signature bears outgrows because of having overreaction as of conditional compulsion(s).

To develop the trait of expression there is a following doodle as a graphotharepy-

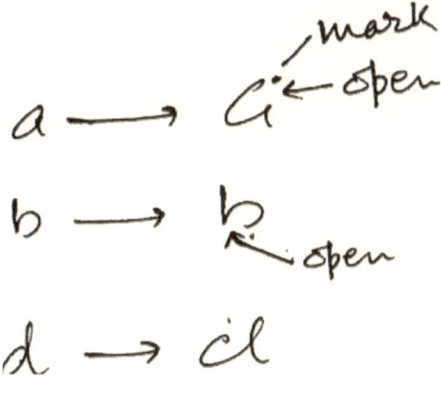

Fig. 2.2.vii

These are open letters at start or at end. It should be practiced with slow speed and marking must be minded at place of their opening. It would be part of handwriting or practiced additionally for 2-5 minutes 4-6 times a day.

(viii) Being weak form of "affirmation" in panic disordered person is common phenomenon. He easily goes for compromising with conditions because of not having proper logic about his own stand on particular topic and condition. If such situations are repeated many times results gradual suppression of basic killer instinct in person. This needs proper satisfaction on ego level and later on the suppressed basic killer instinct become cause of anxiety and regarding particular condition with deep concern of self-security system, which comes in the form of panic attack for few minutes, hours or days. Such person does not have clear mind on his compromises is depicted by handwriting as both acute and circular folds abnormally found in handwriting sample, uphill starts in 'm' and 'n' are observed in handwriting reveals person's intelligence and upper zone of signature shows needle extension. In such person, it is needed to be a strong trait of "strong establishment with known reason in known conditions and subjects". To make it strongly acting the following doodle is suitable as graphotherepy -

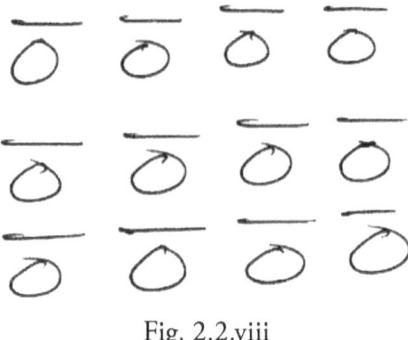

Fig. 2.2.viii

First draw a circle and then secondly line on its upper side. It should be practiced for 5-10 times a day for 2-5 minutes.

(ix) Condition born mental disownity is common problem in panic disordered person. Due to which person deviates from his objective and contemporary tasks. The phenomenon causes person coming of unwanted thoughts in extra prolonged resting phase of mind. It has been described before.

As a graphotharepy person will have to maintain gap of between 0.5 cm. to 1.0 cm among two successive words. This will result not exceeding resting phase. It must not be gap of more than 7 minutes between two successive different conditions.

(x) Panic disordered person must have to better command on coming thoughts from happened events in the past. It is impossible to check all of them to come in mind, so there is only way to command all of on just current relevant ground as per requirement. In such person, there is no management power to overcome that unwanted emotional phenomenon related to the panic attack or causing factors.

There are two way to control such thoughts coming from conditions of past or situation by strong establishment of present reasonable justifications according conditional demand with having astonishing look into of low level intelligence due to which objective attracts person.

Therefore, person has to create the trait of strong establishment on past run conditions. The following doodle as graphotherepy is responsible to create pathway-

(a) It is cross having elongated rightward curved line. The IInd step curved line is much longer than Ist step line. It should be practiced for 2-5 minutes for 5-10 times a day.

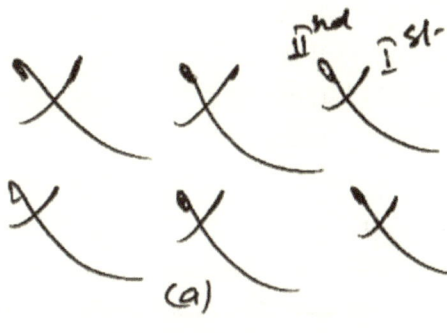

Fig. 2.2. x.a

(b) The next doodle as graphotherapy is in this section is to create the low level of intelligence like young hood logic power to make new look of getting astonished. The graphotharepy is-

Fig. 2.2.x.b

It does not possess the sudden turn anywhere and needs normal speed of practicing. Practice schedule should be 2-5 times for 5-10 times a day on white paper.

(xi) The panic disorder person does not have normal sociality. If he has its proper form but after disorder of panic attack, gradually sociality starts become weaker and many distortion occurs in that form may be either as particular or holistic. Proper sociality provides the person proper objective to think, to work, many grounds of rational exchange and additional matters of consideration and at the same time development of self-accountabilities could be instigator regarding any particular objective and create cause of getting ashamed and causes of fear on which as reaction to be foot back from. Fear and being foot back re also forms of opportunities or may be a part of opportunity management. Therefore, sociality is opportunity, accountability and rationality. All these work together to find out new objective with better presentation. However, mode of presentation is just like playing with double-edged sword. On more possibilities, there are more opportunities and possibilities and on other hand due to inappropriate presentation, person may get shocked on correlation with causes of condition born drawbacks, which leads to result anxiety in from of panic attack. Therefore, panic attack disorder ridden person should have to look for selective sociality. Gradually he should go towards unlimited openness and unselective sociality as well.

Instead of handwriting, sociality is better revealed by signature as the panic disorder ridden person normally has "single unit" of signature. Sociality has characteristic feature in signature as two as or more than two-segmented signatures. As a graphotharepy, the person should has to sign signature in two or more than two segments which must be legible.

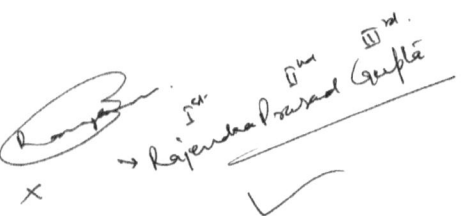

Fig. 2.2.xi

CHAPTER – 3

Obsessive-Compulsive Disorder (OCD)

There are two forms of one disorder. It is often observed sometimes one form is dominated in a person and in other one is not, sometimes both are in dominated form and sometimes it may be observed its balanced form. In psychiatry, no specific reason could be find out behind its balancing order.

A. **Obsession** - The person continuously repeats unwanted absurd, irrational thoughts and imagination in this stage. However, he knows very well about all silliness, meaningless and absurdness of thoughts and imagination. Person wants to get him rid off from all of unwanted emotional malfunctions, but he finds him helpless and such thoughts create too much anxiety in individual through invading mind. According to DSM (IV) there are following facts about the obsession-

   (i)   Obsession is directly related to the ideas, thoughts and images.
   (ii)   Such ideas and thoughts are absurd and meaningless.
   (iii)   Such ideas and thoughts are repetitive and disturb the mental rhythm of person by recurring themselves.
   (iv)   There is no control of person on their invasion or production.

   To classify thought & ideas into mental disorder the criteria added in DSM (IV) that such thoughts must be panic for person, there must be wastage of much more time and thoughts must be cause of obstruction for their daily routine, educational and intellectual works.

B. **Compulsion** – Compulsion is abnormal type of behavioral reaction in which person has to compel to repeat a work many times against his general will. Such actions are not only unexpected but also irrational and irrelevant. Behavior of cleaning again and again, sense of over sanitation, checking lock whether that is locked or not, note down the number of vehicles standing on road side, kleptomania (will to steal anything) pyromania (will to make something catch five) are the examples of compulsion. Compulsion has the facts-

(i) In compulsion person repeats any work again and against his will.

(ii) In compulsion the work done by person are not only unexpected but also irrational and irrelevant.

Forms of obsession – There are five forms-

(i) **Obsessive doubt** - Persistent thought of completed task e.g. room locked or not.

(ii) **Obsessive thinking** - Persistent thoughts concerning events going to be happened in future.

(iii) **Obsessive impulses** - Frequently coming of impulsive thoughts of doing very meanly and general tasks.

(iv) **Obsessive fear** - Fear of doing such task due to losing their confidence. Fear of success is also categorized in this form.

(v) **Obsessive image**- Persistent imaging of concerned events.

Forms of Compulsion- There are two forms-

(i) **Yielding Compulsion** – In this category person feels pressure to do specific irrational work again and again e.g. checking pocket for something special even knowing there is nothing over.

(ii) **Controlling Compulsion** – In this category person tries to overcome his irrational work by countering other irrational work e.g. to nullify the being or coming of snake beating stick loudly or shouting.

Symptoms revealed by handwriting – There are following symptoms of OCD in the handwriting-

(i) Abnormally there are additional out growth in handwriting and signatures seen. The out growth is additional extension of letters and signature is made more than their basic need. The extension indicates the strong intension of covering more matters or conditional factors around him anyway. However, the objective of covering the matters is formed contemporarily which are prolonged for long time specifically. It is found sometimes person gets stucked into that strong situation for long duration. This is another cause of anxiety. Gradually the person gets into the habit of that particular situation or condition. The phenomenon habitually repeats on own self and creates severe anxiety. The outgrowth is efforts done by the person to nullify those of all causes with replacing other causes or conditional factors, which yield anxiety.

However, the OCD suffering person has better capability of thinking on any particular subject and on objectives in comparison to normal person. However, he also thinks conditions and their factors are not in support of his target of achieving system and if that would be as he thinks then his performance would have in quite appropriate way. On thinking, form of all concerns come is form of anxiety. Due to not being supportive according to what the person wants, the conditions and circumstances leave more factors to cause anxiety and later on all become much more disliked rather than whole conditions and situations. The negative attitude about conditions and circumstances depicted by handwriting as fluctuation observed in alignment of handwriting and at the same time, the significant feature curved alignment occurred because of being condition-based confidence that does not support to their objective. Some letters of handwriting are seen compressed from upper side due to much more negative impact of conditional factors. Placement of letters is not in proper fashion due to having variation in conditional impact. The curved alignment is also observed in signature

(ii)   OCD suffering person shows the curved alignment in his handwriting sample. Firstly, the alignment goes up then starts becoming downward going. The straight alignment of words in handwriting reveals the mode of considering the factors as on their criteria towards getting some specific output in about all condition or situations accordingly. In OCD the curved alignment depicts the consideration of procedure and output are not just normal. The mode of consideration is in over form to find some better output. Straight alignment and then downward going alignment in next step is interpretation of unsuccessful procedure of getting positive outputs, which is significant and directly damages person's "over confidence" like falling in deep ditch from High Mountain.

(iii)   The OCD stricken person shows loop in lower part of 's & S' which reveals trait of responsibility feeling in handwriting. Most of persons have its abnormal exception intended to form loop but not make. The reason behind this phenomenon is that person wants to share his extra burden of responsibilities and due to obsession and compulsion born deviations he wants to be freed from the feeling of responsibilities which is reflected in handwriting as intention to make loop in lower part of "s & S" up to some extent. All factors related to responsibility are always kept under person's concern cause anxiety and that comes out as obsessive compulsive disorder (OCD).

(iv) All OCD people show high elevation in the letter of their handwriting because of doing extra mental work. It has been explained before what OCD has malfunctions about thoughts, ideas and imaginations. The elevations of letters reveal the process of coming thoughts and ideas and high elevation of letters also reveal the more frequency of coming ideas and thoughts on a particular subject or topic. The elevation also determines the form of factors and their perception about references on correlation with other traits. In person, the thoughts and ideas are of unique type on any single and particular topic come for long duration leads to cause compulsion of coming again.

Some OCD suffering person shows "hanging accessories of letters", which is the significant feature of panic disorder in handwriting sample. Therefore, this is possibility of panic attack in OCD persons or having some part of panic disorder converts into compulsion. However, I could not find any OCD person who has been suffering from panic attack along so far.

Obsessive compulsive disorder =   curved alignment + loop in lower part of s and P + out growth in letters and signature + Abnormal elevations in letters.

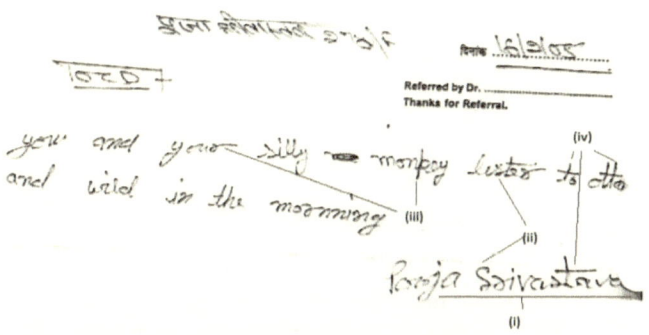

Fig. 2.3

A. Important Traits To Be Considered Accordingly While Making Report -

Towards reforming personality traits through intrapersonal communication by neural pathways of those via brain learning, personality research report is required as mentioned earlier and to prepare therapeutic personality research report consist of all instructions to be communicated and state of mind along. There are following important traits to be considered according to the unique personality revealed by handwriting sample for communication, consulting guidance or counseling towards empowering personality traits would lead to mental empowerment with cure. Well, considering these all are not mandatory and strictly depend on what handwriting reveals, which may let permit to add new traits not mentioned here. The traits are characterized here by as handwriting depicted by chronic psychopaths. On missing any or many characteristics, change in guidance format will occur accordingly. Well during preparation of therapeutic personality research report, these following suggestions should be kept in mind. If person is on self-cure, he must prepare his therapeutic research report this way towards curing. Because of being unique personality, report will be unique so, uniqueness must be kept under deep consideration and differences should be identified according to form, presence and absence of characteristics -

1. Better and positive thinking about works, conditions and circumstances will helpful keep person away from anxiety caused by these. There is no mean of negative thoughts because person has negative attitude about these concerns depicted in handwriting as –

   (i)   More space is taken by loops made by down strokes.
   (ii)   Fluctuation observed in alignment of handwriting.
   (iii) Some letters observed as compressed from upside.
   (iv)   Placements of letters are not observed in proper and regular fashion.
   (v)   Signature goes up first then down.

2. On most be liked matters person should be strong affirmative on those and he should tried to give those strong look as he wants because wills of person deeply and negatively affected by circumstances revealed by handwriting as –

   (i) Words are completed with slow speed.
   (ii) Letters are completed carefully.
   (iii) Tradition of furnishing letters is minded carefully.

3. Person should do special works during special occasions. This is very necessary because the confidence of person is up in initial stages of working and in other conditions also therefore this should be used in positive way. The trait is depicted in handwriting as –

   (i) Handwriting and signature goes up first.
   (ii) Accessories of letters smaller in first word but not forwarded as such.

4. Regarding any work, condition or subject if person feels any complication, he should try to find their easy way either they are positive or negative because person has more perplexes between works and their contemporary aim creates some sort of complications handwriting depicts as –

   (i) Lesser differences between A and a, C and c, E and e ... and so on.

5. Between two successive conditions person should keep gap of 10 to 15 minutes because he does not keep appropriate gap between two successive condition which results condition born mental overlapping which is revealed in handwriting as –

   (i) Very lesser gap observed between two successive words of handwriting.

6. Person should imagine pleasure about coming condition if could not he must find out points of pleasures according him because person has strong sense of danger is revealed by handwriting as –

(i) There are many sudden breaks observed in handwriting.
(ii) Any or many letters of handwriting are tried to decorate more by overwriting.
(iii) No regular gap is among words.

7. Reading news paper would be very helpful for the OCD person because he has single dominant subject to think and newspaper provides him to think more subject to think more.

8. OCD person should conclude his works or campaigns proudly because person has strong and reactive ego with proud but there is no correlation between both of them regarding working the characteristics of unhealthy ego revealed by handwriting as –

(i) No significant difference between size of capital letters and small letters.
(ii) Upward going signature then downward.
(iii) Disturbed rhythm observed in both big and small letters.

9. OCD person should not go under self-pressure to do this he should pay proper respect to his own will because of having conditional pressure is revealed by handwriting as –

(i) Uniformity of handwriting is lesser disturbed than regularity.
(ii) Speed of writing is less than normal.
(iii) More pressure imposed on paper by the pen.
(iv) Some words are not well furnished.

10. To keep self away from the negative thoughts person should respond all negative subjects also in respect of positive attitude.

11. For OCD person being any of prejudice or persistent is very necessary but he must make his mentality after proper testing of subject. Complete mind set must be on data whatever he gets from subject. The characteristics of prejudice is depicted by handwriting as –

(i) The rhythm of handwriting is badly disturbed.

(ii) Manic or straight upright handwriting observed.

12. The OCD person should react after some times on any subject i.e. he should wait for 2-3 minutes but should not be exceeded by 30 minutes because person keeps himself always in solution seeking of problems in the form of obsession. The taken time makes person available more topics within the topic for consideration. The trait is depicted in handwriting as –

(i) Specified deformations are seen in handwriting.

(ii) Signature is bigger.

(iii) Signature is in two or more than two parts.

(iv) In handwriting "n" hump is observed.

13. OCD person must not be lonely because most of unnecessary problems are come under person's consideration that enhances obsession. The trait revealed by handwriting as –

(i) Long down strokes observed in handwriting.

(ii) The upper zone stroke is observed in handwriting.

14. Maintaining daily diary will be more helpful regarding positivity about self accountability related to new thoughts and ideas because OCD person has strong trait of coming new thoughts and ideas. The trait is revealed by handwriting as –

(i) Elevated letters are observed in handwriting.

(ii) Slight manic form of handwriting.

(iii) Slow speed of handwriting.

B. Graphotherapies - There are three doodles as a graphotherapy –

(i) The OCD person does not look for the opportunities to find the way of their target apart from what he has adopted even if contemporary or goal of life. He has to go for proper under consideration of all types of factor available anywhere regarding his target on adopted way. The strong effort regarding such issues he would have to start the learning to command the condition and the pathways of such trait will get created and then their confidence will shift to the basic instinct from the condition. The doodle is –

$$\int \int \int \int \int$$

Fig. 2.3.i.a

It should be practiced with slow speed for 2-5 minutes 4-6 times a day.

a. At the same time for better command the conditions and circumstances, the OCD person must have clear ambition regarding his outputs of campaigns and works that would correlate with their contemporary target, goal and to create such neural pathways, the signature of the person must be upward going.

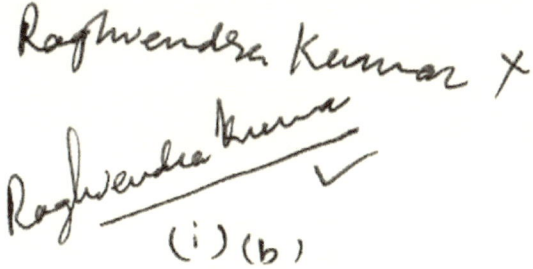

Fig. 2.3.i b

(ii)   To strengthen his confidence he should practice another doodle. In fact all types of conditions do not possess extra properties regarding presentation. Therefore, the person needs some sort of strong ground on his ambitious functions.

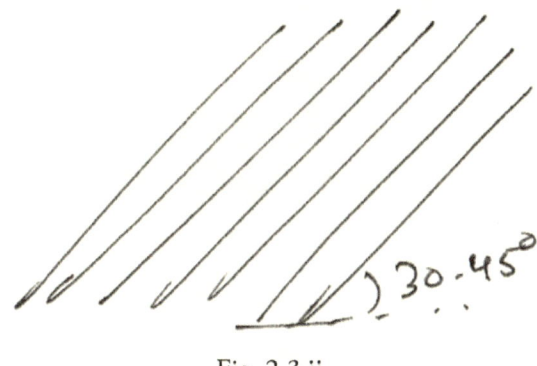

Fig. 2.3.ii

These are the upward going lines on slanted on 30-45°. It should be practiced with high speed as much as possible for just 2-5 minutes 5-10 times a day.

(iii)   OCD person is badly affected by his unfavorable "conditioned factors" due to which natural will is directly suppressed. The person takes extra care on matter of his own will. The suppression of wills and process of that both are sever cause of anxiety come out in the form of obsessive compulsive disorder. The mental status depicted by handwriting as words are completed with slow speed carefully and furnished traditionally paying some more intention. Therefore, the matters, which are liked most by the OCD suffering person and on that issue he should be strong affirmative. They must have to give them some special look by own efforts.

To get this trait person have to be some move creative on thinking level as well as working, all works concerning this trait should be original as much as possible and it is tried not to be copied form others along. It must be determined by those thoughts come alive in working, for reformation or creation of this trait, this is the doodle as graphotherapy -

Fig. 2.3.iii

Well, it stands for creating the engineering creative mind on correlation with other traits but also have move suitable for thinking like that and converts all those thoughts into creations. It should be practiced for 2-5 minutes and 5-10 times a day.

(iv) The OCD ridden person has better confidence in initial stages of any campaign or condition. After some times, confidence becomes started shifting on conditions and their factors. The status formed because of being non-supportive conditional factors. To get rid of "confidence shift" problem, person has to utilize their time in specified mode. The confidence shift, reflected in the handwriting as handwriting and signature go up then become down and the accessories of letters are not seen regularly fashioned because of many types of obstruction are created strong with imposition on personality by unfavorable conditions.

Therefore, the OCD person should have to do some special work to be special time. To make it come develop there is following doodle as graphtharapy –

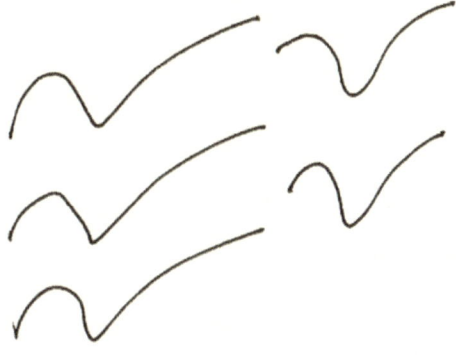

Fig. 2.3.iv

The doodle is suitable for creating pathways intended to use available conditional factors in the favors according to person. The single doodle is upward going. It should be practiced with slow speed in initial time and gradually the speed should be practiced 2-5 minutes and 4-6 times a day.

(v)   The OCD ridden suffering persons have much maze between works and their contemporary aim, which creates some sort of specified complications. The trait depicted in handwriting as bigger loop in letter "a" and in respect of 'a' the letter 'e' is quite irrelevant, due to repetition of irrational phenomenon, the frequency occurs in regular fashion, which revealed in handwriting as the irregularity in deformation is observed in definite type.

Such person should have to look for the easiest way on complications or complicated matter in greater context of concept based working either those are positive or negative. To reform this trait as graphotherapy they should write alphabets like primary standard having their full and better form of conscious mind –

Fig. 2.3.v

Loop of such letter must be in almost homogenous form. At least 2 times a day should have to be written. The speed of writing must be slow.

(vi) In most OCD stricken person the "condition born mental overlapping" is observed commonly which is reflected in handwriting as less than 0.5 cm gap among two successive words. This is due to paying much more intention on their contemporary target that is the main cause of creation of anxiety in person. Therefore, person needs to maintain the gap between two words .5 to 1.0 cm as a graphotherapy.

Handwriting of some people shows both symptoms the lesser gap (condition born mental overlapping) and more gap (condition born mental disownity). In starting stage of handwriting they show mental overlapping and later on that starts showing condition born mental disownity, so as graphotherapy they also need to maintain the gap between 0.5 cm to 1.00 cm. Along with practicing graphotharepy the interval of 7-15 minutes between two successive conditions must be maintained by person suffering from OCD. For mental overlapping persons the interval must not be less than 7 minutes between two successive conditions.

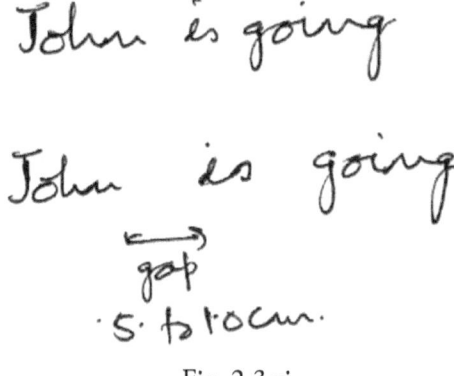

Fig. 2.3.vi

(vii) Pleasant environment and pleasure both are necessary for OCD striken person to make light the circumstances as he pays much more intention on their contemporary aim or target up to creation of anxiety, which results facing much more irrational thoughts, ideas on compulsion level to do irrational works. There is existence of either yielding compulsion or controlling compulsion and then their justifications. In connection to all these three mental phenomena, make person too much serious about coming condition. The form of this trait is revealed in handwriting as presence of many sudden breaks in many letters and no regular gap between two words. The sudden break in letters is made due to paying extra intention on their unwanted conditions and conditional factors and irregular gap is due to irregularities in process of coming ideas and thoughts.

Therefore, there is much more need of making person happy by creating new trait. Because of having strong danger feelings and danger about the coming conditions, the mode of perception must not be serious. To create the trait of happiness, there is following suitable doodle as graphotherapy –

Fig. 2.3.vii

This is upward going connected many "u" on 30-45⁰ slant. The elevation should be kept in mind that is must not be less than 0.5 cm. It should be practical with high speed 2-5 times and 5-10 times a day. It also covers trait of intelligence in positive way. Practicing this graphotherapy, person should read newspapers daily. The matter may be selective according to him.

(viii) The OCD suffering person has strong unhealthy ego and proud and due to being of those person does not go easily for compromising with conditions and situations as per demand. There should be a correlation between person's healthy ego and their circumstances. There is no such a way is seen to the person. Another type of correlation must be between their works and their conclusions. On damaging person's healthy ego by any unfavorable condition or conditional factor, such hitting procedure also disturbs the trait of proud. The healthy ego is revealed by handwriting as – first letter of handwriting seen quite bigger in size, gradual increment of letters and disturbs correlation revealed in handwriting as curved alignment of handwriting and signature due to "confidence shift" and disturbed rhythm of handwriting, it is depicted by some letters.

There are three doodles as graphotherapy –

a. It is found that the OCD person does not have sufficient ability to select the worthy options or like such from in their circumstances. Frequently coming ideas and thoughts are quite irrational and that is why person is not able to pay proper intention on such factors for campaign or objective. Therefore, there is dare need to person that he has to shift his intention from obsession and compulsion to meaningful and worthy factors regarding objectives and concern contemplation. The graphotherapy for this is –

Fig. 2.3.viii.a

It should be practiced with slow speed initially and after sometimes it should be increased gradually. The pattern of practice is 2-5 minutes and 5-10 times a day.

b. Factors and causes repeat themselves repeatedly frequently. Person does have concluding concept of any matter, campaign or subject. Once if any one of them gets started then that gets prolonged endlessly. This is also one of the major causes of person's anxiety converts into OCD. It is must to have the concept and to create this trait there is following doodle as a graphotharapy –

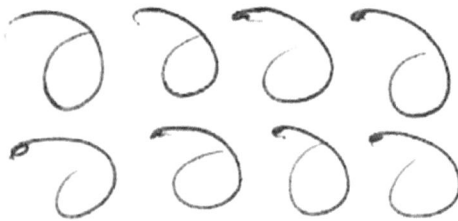

Fig. 2.3.viii.b

It should be mind that end is must and extended beyond it upper cover. This is the most suitable not to extend factors more than need. Practice pattern is 2-5 min. for 4-6 times a day.

c. OCD suffering person does not know the reasons of their anxiety. Due to anxiety person has already damaged their trait of establishment and therefore, he uses his mind much more to find out the cause of them. Indeed, this is a meaningless effort because of stimulation of such obsession and compulsions are produced by contemporary circumstances. Therefore, it is necessary for OCD stricken person that he has keep better and strong establishment in all conditions and circumstances strongly and in passive way. To recreate such trait in person, this doodle is responsible for "strong self-establishment with known reason in known conditions with subjects". However, during initial stages the OCD suffering person should face the known condition as much as possible. The doodle as graphotherapy is –

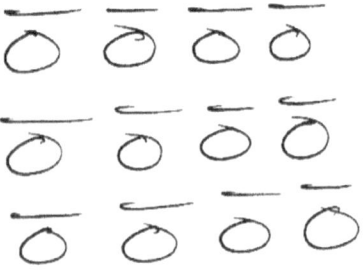

Fig. 2.3.viii.c

It should be practiced with slow speed for 2-5 minutes and 4-6 times a day.

(ix) In OCD suffering person loneliness feeling is common problem. This is due to "centralizing self" on the problems. In lonely places, there is strong possibility of getting him increased anxiety and commonly he wants to think of their obsessions and compulsions without obstruction. The trait of loneliness is revealed by handwriting as there are long down strokes are observed and thinking property on OCD and its cause revealed as the upper zone strokes found which indicate the mental over activeness in the center of their contemplation. The following doodle as graphotherapy that hits the contemplation trait to make it blunt up to some extent and to weak the loneliness –

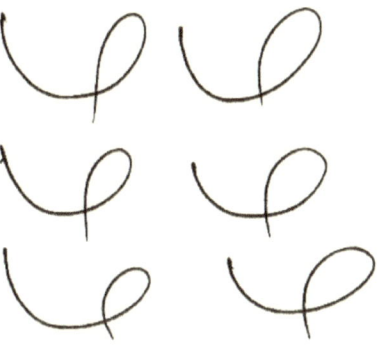

Fig. 2.3.ix

It should be practiced with slow speed for 2-5 minutes 4-6 times a day.

UNIT - 3

SCHIZOPHRENIA

Chapter – 1

Schizophrenia

Schizophrenia is the most serious mental disorder commonly known as "insane or mad" in layman's language. It is a disorder of highly disturbed thinking and troubled mood. There is a disorder in thinking of stricken person that taking place of concentration disability on particular because of subjective or objective with developing irrelevant concepts. The person shows his expressions as very incapable to regarding both concerns. In this disorder there is originations of false perception and false believe dwell along in the person. Because of that, there is more enough difficulties in understanding realities and at the same time serious problems related to speech, emotional expression and disabilities, all phenomena correlate each other to move person toward compete disturbance.

It is define as "Schizophrenia is a group psychotic disorders characterized by major disturbance in thoughts, emotions and behavior- disordered thinking in which ideas are not logically related, faulty perception and attention create bizarre disturbance in motor activities and flat or inappropriate affect". - Division & Neale: *Abnormal Psychology*, 1996, p. 389

It is the serious most disorder in which complete personality of person becomes fully disturbed. There are following significant feature of schizophrenia –

(i)   Person gets disturbed on the stage while logical sequence and rhythmic pattern of reasonable thinking become ended.

(ii)   There is no more cognition of realities remains in person just because of formation of virtual world takes place fulfilled with strong delusion and hallucinations.

(iii)   The person seems to be like more living in his virtual world, so it is quite natural breaking his up social relationships.

(iv)   Not even only his thinking and emotion but also behavior are completely disorganized.

Clinical symptoms of schizophrenia - There are three types of symptoms in abnormal psychology-

(a) positive symptoms

(b) negative symptoms

(c) psychomotor symptoms

(a) **Positive symptoms-** The meaning of positive symptom is showing off psychological excesses by person. The symptoms categorized in this section, are disorganized thinking and speech, hallucination and inappropriate effects.

    (i)   **Delusion** - Delusion is designed by such false belief in spite of even events being proved false, person does not agree to accept all proofs regarding that particular context. Some schizophrenic people prominently have single strong delusion but it is observed some people with many delusions. According to American psychiatric association (APA 1994) in schizophrenia, the most important fact is being of 'delusion of persecution' but in others 'delusion of reference', 'grandiosity' and 'control' are observed. Due to delusion, behavior of schizophrenic person may be enough more violent.

    Delusion of Persecution- False belief is that, person is discriminated by plan, invaded, threaten, or being perplexed intentionally by someone else.

Delusion of Reference- Believing falsely person adds his specified behavior like someone talking about himself using every medium of communication.

Delusion of Grandiosity- Being false belief as big mentor, historical personality and religious leader.

Delusion of being Controlled- False belief is like that someone else controls his emotions, thinking and functions.

(ii) **Hallucination-** Perception of any particular object or external world in its absence is hallucination. Well, there are many types of hallucinations observed in schizophrenia but most significant is auditory hallucination. The schizophrenic person percepts or experiences such sounds and voices from outside of his head would be of many or single acquainted or non-acquainted (new) man criticizing, treating or complimenting him.

In association of this, the other hallucinations are tactile hallucination, somatic hallucination, visual hallucination and olfactory hallucination are also observed in some schizophrenic people. In some of them both stages of hallucination and delusion are often observed.

(iii) **Disorganized Speech and Thinking -** The disorganized speech is designed as in, which the person has loose correlation between established thoughts and mode of thinking regarding present situations. Such people change their subject in such hastened way that the listening person could not get all happenings instantaneously what schizophrenic expresses. Such types of people ask inappropriate, irrational and irrelevant questions and even respond in the same way. They show formal thinking disorder as persevering and in rhyme in frequent way.

(iv) **Inappropriate Affect -** Many schizophrenic persons show quite different type of emotions quite irrelevant to conditions and situations. They often express their great grief on getting pleasant information or something similar like that. They become happy when they are given unpleasant information. Not only such, there are inappropriate 'shifts of mood' are also observed in them.

(b) Negative symptoms- There are following negative symptoms of schizophrenia –

(i) **Poverty of Speech** - There is various types of disorder related to the speech are observed in schizophrenic person. Schizophrenic person often uses minimum words to answer and after long gap. Many times, he does not respond. There are much more blocks could be mentioned easily in their statements as their thoughts disappear from his memory. Talks of such people are throughout meaningless.

(ii) **Blunt and Flat Affects** - Some schizophrenic people show blunt emotions in comparison to normal people such people show lesser emotions, sadness, happiness or other affect. Some people does not show any emotion and affect called flat effects of schizophrenia.

(iii) **Disturbance in Volition** – Because of having distorted and deformed own world, various changes occur in willing of such schizophrenic person. Apathy, lack of energy, interest and disability to complete any work etc. are generally observed in them. These symptoms are mostly observed in chronic schizophrenic people. The ambivalent mood is also found in some schizophrenic people.

(iv) **Disturbed Relationship with External World** – Generally, the schizophrenic person make himself detach emotionally and socially from their external world and get lost in their world of imagination and thought. Due to being irrational and distorted thoughts, it assists withdrawal more keeping them away from realities.

(c) Psychomotor symptoms- Many schizophrenic persons also show psychomotor symptoms. These are specific psycho muscular bizarre poses and forms of symptoms are repetitive and often seem to be purposeful as well. The behavior shown by such people are quite surprising, ridiculous and in extreme form. As symptoms are repetitive and generally seem to be purposive, are in fact keep person on the edge of danger repeatedly. Sometimes psychomotor symptom of schizophrenia gets prolonged to its extreme form that is known as catatonia. In this category the most common symptoms are -

Catatonia stepper	–	Shows unresponsive
Catatonia rigidity	–	Continue its posture which is specific.
Catatonia posturing	–	Bizarre body posture
Catatonic excitement	–	Extreme violent stage of person.

Diagnosing the schizophrenia

From the very beginning, diagnosis of schizophrenia is quite disputed subject because its every symptom is also observed in other mental disorders, traumatic stress and somatic diseases in any. More over in DSM-IV there are 4 criteria to diagnose the schizophrenia –

(i) Person who has been showing the symptoms of schizophrenia for last six months or more, at least one month out of these six months should definitely be active phase of basic delusion, hallucination, disorganized speech, catatonic symptoms and negative symptoms. Rest of period may be of prodormal or residual phase.

(ii) There must have been deterioration in self-care, social relationships etc.

(iii) If person has experienced manic or depressive form, then must have before or after schizophrenia or it must be for very short period than that of schizophrenia.

(iv) The schizophrenia must not be due to substance use of medical condition like brain tumor, brain trauma or deficiency of vitamin B_{12} etc.

Types of schizophrenia

According DSM-IV (1994) there are five types of schizophrenia –

1- Disorganized schizophrenia
2- Catatonic schizophrenia
3- Paranoid schizophrenia
4- Undifferentiated schizophrenia
5- Residual schizophrenia

1. **Disorganized Schizophrenia-** The significant features of disorganized schizophrenia are confusion, incoherence and flat affects. In this type of schizophrenia the confusion and delusion are significantly observed and at the same time sexual, hypochondriac, religious and persecutory are poorly organized which disturb complete routine. Because of that person has problem in doing his all routine works related to his life. Person has strong feeling of body deterioration. In such person, the flatness and perceptions are much strong that his social isolation and withdrawal become stronger as well. Therefore, such person shows silly behavior like giggling without reason.

2. **Catatonic schizophrenia-** It has all symptoms of psychomotor symptoms as described earlier.

3. **Paranoid Schizophrenia** - Most important symptom of this category is being of strong and systematic delusion and auditory hallucination. There is significantly presence of delusion of persecution and but that delusion of hideously, delusion of grandiosity, delusions of reference are also found. More over many auditory hallucinations are observed in such person and due to which his delusion stages become stronger. On asking about such hallucination, the person becomes violent and shows anxiety. In some person, delusion of grandiosity is found prominently with liking loneliness along.

4. **Undifferentiated Schizophrenia** - This is category of such disordered person in which the schizophrenia could not be categorized even being symptom of schizophrenia and symptoms

disappear for very short term, condition is referred as 'acute undifferentiated schizophrenia'. Since disorder of schizophrenia gets started gradually and becomes persistent then referred as "Chronic undifferentiated schizophrenia".

5. **Residual schizophrenia** – This is categorized by such person who does not follow the criteria of schizophrenia completely but they are observed symptoms of schizophrenia. This way the acute symptoms of schizophrenia become decreased in number and intensity but still remains in residual form. According to DSM-IV there are following symptoms of this type of schizophrenia –

    I.   Social relation and withdrawal
    II.   Impairment in social participation
    III.   Bizarre behavior
    IV.   Severe impairment in social participation and in self-grooming
    V.   Inappropriate blunts or flats emotional expression.
    VI.   Prissier or magical thinking
    VII.   Unusual perceptual emotional expressions
    VIII.   Apathy and lack of initiative

As there course of schizophrenia concerns it differs person to person. There are –

(i)   Prodromal phase
(ii)   Active phase
(iii)   Residual phase.

In prodromal phase the symptoms of schizophrenia are not visible clearly but the person seems to be in process of beginnings destruction of personality that results deterioration occurred in routine of his normal life like getting isolated from the society, disability to perform his duties and responsibility, bizarre habits like collection of garbage, ignorance of hygienic customs etc. The strong and clear symptoms are observed in active phase. The person's mental condition seems to be looking very stressful with disturbing routine life. Both types of symptoms positive and negative are observed in active phase. Residual phase shows the symptoms of coming back prodromal phase. However, the serious positive symptoms of active phase are not observed but continuous deterioration of personality still remain with emotions and disability to perform.

According to strange (1992) "only 25% percent become cured hardly but not completely that residual impairment still remains which may come in active phase any time in future.

The reason behind problem of not being cure is reformation or formations of new neural pathways of personality traits do not take place in proper way through intrapersonal communication directly related to this disorder. It is found many of person of paranoid schizophrenics becomes cured without medication because of taking place of formation of new neural pathways by chance as there are infinite factors in circumstances can insist initiation of reformation – formation incidentally. Therefore, the fact comes out that formation or reformation of new neural pathways of traits through intrapersonal communication is rather more important than medication. Role of medicine is only to bring patient out from apathetic stage of attack to normal conscious stage. Then it is very necessary to provide treatment of intrapersonal communication towards brain learning to reform old neural pathways or create new neural pathways of active personality traits based on therapeutic handwriting analysis based personality research report, should be started towards curing with proper mental empowerment.

Symptom of Paranoid Schizophrenia in Handwriting – Severe stages and panic attacks are beyond the limit of Emotional Engineering. However, paranoid schizophrenia is curable even if it is diagnosed in its early stages or in residual phase. Commonly it is found in strong self-centered personality having person and in those who are extremely sensitive towards their conditions and circumstances consider all factors according to own self are more endangered because of using "security system" in extreme on correlation with trait of logic power. There are following symptoms –

(i)   Size of letters plays important role in formation of hallucination as a disorder. Tinny size of handwriting and abnormally big size of handwriting both have strong possibilities of delusion and hallucination. The tinny handwriting reveals person is self-centered and due to which person considers most of conditional factors would be related to him in "selective form". In this connection, the negative factors are excessively considered. This is the base of delusion. However, factors are coming to be under his consideration, are quite selective and due to paying more intention on negativities that may become internally reactive, in particular form.

The person who writes bigger, considers enough more conditional factors from the circumstances. For such person normally condition and circumstances are most disturbing because of being those all seem to be as a strong security concerns and tackled on security measures. Therefore, "efforts of overcoming" all concerns of security create extreme stress through various ways of itself and some other conditional factors by any mean. The factors created by those conditions and circumstances are also disturbing and does not let minimize created stress. Big letters reveals this all phenomenon. Negative factors are also paid more intention with respect of others.

(ii)   The most significant feature of paranoid schizophrenia is "broken and imperfect" letters of words in handwriting and signature both. Breaking may take place at anywhere in the letter. This property is commonly observed in handwriting sample reveals withdrawal of the person from society and preferring isolation. In Hindi language, it is observed that marking of vowels are used not in perfect way. In many cases their direction are changed even may be reverse, which is quite unacceptable and considered as blunders mistakes. In English language some parts or any part of letter become disappeared due to strong working of unwanted system and creating system of hallucination and with isolation along. These symptoms would be common at some place of the handwriting repeatedly. Number of this abnormality directly depicts acuteness of disorder. In some paranoid schizophrenic people, it is not shown by handwriting but anomaly shown in completing processes of words as breaks. Symptoms of this abnormality is clearly shown in mother language. Well imperfection abnormality of letters in marking accessories may be as misplaced i-dot at any place of handwriting or some other place but not common. This due to disturbance in normal function, invasion of hallucination occurs.

(iii)　All paranoid schizophrenic people show abnormal outgrowth in letters and words. At many places those outgrowths seems as suddenly stopped. This is because of prolonged interchange between systemic activation of delusion or hallucination and original personality of person as he was before. The complete outgrowth depicts extra reactivates of person where as sudden stop or break is just due to activation of controlling system on hallucination caused reactions. Because of being the another form of active ego, delusion comes in commanding role with strong wants of keeping reactions in commanding position but hallucination, which is caused by panic then ego gets converted into delusion by virtual gain of more related conditional factors on according to egoistic demand to nullify the hallucination. All originated by conditional factors panic circumstances. Such systematic conflict uses almost whole personality system results paranoid schizophrenia.

Paranoid Schizophrenia – Big or Tinny letters + Imperfection in Letters or words + Disconnected Letters (on getting isolated & withdrawal) + Abnormal Outgrowths of Letters.

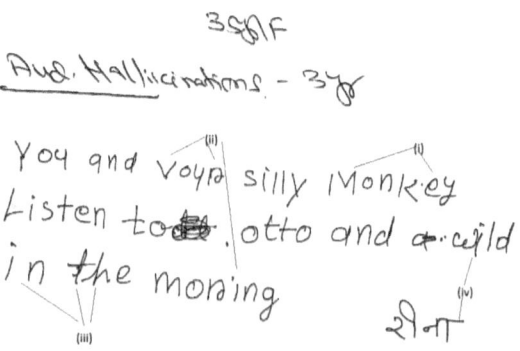

Fig. 3.1

A. **Important Traits To Be Considered Accordingly While Making Report -**

Towards reforming personality traits through intrapersonal communication by neural pathways of those via brain learning, personality research report is required as mentioned earlier and to prepare therapeutic personality research report consist of all instructions to be communicated and state of mind along. There are following important traits to be considered according to the unique personality revealed by handwriting sample for communication, consulting guidance or counseling towards empowering personality traits would lead to mental empowerment with cure. Well, considering these all are not mandatory and strictly depend on what handwriting reveals, which may let permit to add new traits not mentioned here. The traits are characterized here by as handwriting depicted by chronic psychopaths. On missing any or many characteristics, change in guidance format will occur accordingly. Well during preparation of therapeutic personality research report, these following suggestions should be kept in mind. If person is on self-cure, he must prepare his therapeutic research report this way towards curing. Because of being unique personality, report will be unique so, uniqueness must be kept under deep consideration and differences should be identified according to form, presence and absence of characteristics -

1. Person suffering from paranoid schizophrenia should determine his exact position and situation and conditional status. The process of determination should be easy and on some light efforts. Most of the concerns should be included related to him because person has problem of perfection about his positioning. The problem is revealed in handwriting as –

   (i) Some letters of handwriting and their accessories are misplaced because of severe conditional fear.
   (ii) Vibration is observed in handwriting and signature.
   (iii) Slow speed of handwriting.

(iv) Unnecessary deformation noted in most of the words and letters observed as not perfect.

(v) No regular alignment is observed in handwriting.

2. Person should stand just in front of mirror, which mirrors your full figure and watch yourself for ½ to 1 an hour because of watching the impact of ideas and thoughts come in the mind of person without proper rational process and that is completely out of control of the person. This is revealed in handwriting as –

(i) There are more and abnormal circular folds in handwriting holding long strokes.

(ii) Abnormally very lesser speed of handwriting.

(iii) Gap among two successive words are not regular and disturbed abnormally.

3. Such people must keep themselves away from serious matters, subjects e.g. serious TV episodes (Soap opera), literatures etc. as person affected by those matters which are provided by his own likings. There are high possibilities of being those in negative form according to the person. This is revealed by handwriting as –

(i) In handwriting the capital and small letters have same differences as person does not do efforts to dominate the condition that is why person feels maximum conditional factors important.

(ii) Letters are completed in irregular fashion.

(iii) Abnormal circular folds in handwriting are observed.

(iv) There are many abnormal changes in handwriting in bending or turns.

4. Paranoid schizophrenic person must recognize his own will and must give proper respect and he must not get suggestions from others because wills of person are badly affected and due

to which he survives as distorted factor of willing system. The trait depicted in handwriting as –

(i) Words are carefully completed and carefully maintained its trend of furnishing.

5. Person must have system of repeating respectful and pleasant moments because of being fear factors in very dangerous form as a system which is reflected in handwriting as –

(i) Abnormally no sudden break is observed in handwriting.
(ii) Some letters of handwriting are tried to decorate more.
(iii) Irregularity observed in gap between successive words.

6. Being positive for every work makes person more useful for the social system having proper importance because person has dangerous attitude regarding one or many aspects which is revealed in handwriting as –

(i) More area covered by loops made by down stroke.
(ii) Fluctuation observed in alignment.
(iii) Placements of accessories of letters are not in proper and regular way.

7. Ill will for any one kept by person must convert all into goodwill because will of person are badly affected by negative conditional factors that results creation factors compel person for giving serious respond. This reflected in handwriting as –

(i) Extra care of letters in handwriting.

8. The paranoid schizophrenic person must keep himself away from all types of prejudices because person is selective prejudice on same subject special for him that would be either positive or negative. The reason behind it is due to there is strong

correlation between ego and related particular factor. This is depicted by handwriting as –

(i) Some specific types of letter furnishing fashion or style are repeated more than one time in handwriting sample.
(ii) Lack of manic form in handwriting.

9. Being humbleness in appropriate amount of paranoid schizophrenic person is very necessary because person is not humble and that is why he gives hard over reaction. The trait is revealed in handwriting as –

(i) Abnormally made circular folds are observed in handwriting.
(ii) The opening and closing of relevant letters are not regular fashion. This is because of strong negative feelings, undefined situations and expressiveness regarding particular context on subconscious mind.
(iii) Many deformations in relevant letters are observed as part of those.

10. Paranoid schizophrenic person should not talk about any one especially negative. Because of having high possibilities of imposition of other mentality on his own is depicted by handwriting as –

(i) Some letters of handwriting are completed abnormally.
(ii) Abnormal acute folds observed in handwriting.
(iii) Many abnormal bending in letters of handwriting are observed.

11. A service of any elder one without selfishness plays important role in crushing unhealthy ego of the person as person has inside him. This trait is identified on trait of humbleness. The will also make person more humble.

12. All concerned circumstances and conditions must be favorable to the person because person is very much rudely over reactive and may be with violation. This depicted in handwriting as –

(i) Blunt end in 't' and 'a'

(ii) Loop of 'd', 'b' and 'B' are made just lower to the half or on the half.

(iii) Loop or type of loop may be made in starting of the signature.

(iv) Speed of handwriting is considerably very slow because of considering all unfavorable and not rest of all extra conditional factors. Types of conditional factors are already established in the mind of person.

13. Person must take time to respond because of being over reactive and this way person can keep himself under control.

B. GRAPHOTHERAPIES – There is following set of graphotherapies to get rid of paranoid schizophrenia (Auditory hallucination) may also be prescribed with psychiatric treatment towards fast recovery.

(i) The person of paranoid schizophrenia has severe problem of perfection, observed in handwriting as misplacement, or disappearance of any or many important part of letter. Such person could not percept normally any object or subject because of being too strong self. This is observed in the form of mal-perception in at random way. The symptoms are observed in handwriting as most of person has very slow speed of writing due to paying much intention, which results abnormal presentation, depicted in handwriting as distorted letters. Such deformations are seen unnecessary but compulsion of person's improper presentation. Alignment of handwriting goes downward gradually because of lacking system of confidence or having loose form of confidence system and handwriting of schizophrenic person does not show disturbed alignment enough. The reason behind it is being manic of schizophrenic person. Such person also has disorder of mania. Very slow speed of handwriting is also responsible to cause the problem of perfection, which reveals paying much intention on conditions and factors yielded.

Therefore, such person should have to determine the exact situation and conditional status. The procedure must be based on some light efforts. In this process all references should be included. There are two graphotherapies-

(a) The schizophrenic person has to draw just standing lines on white paper for getting exact position in conditions and situation.

Fig. 3.1.i.a

It should be practiced with normal speed or high speed and length must not be less than 1.5 cm. The duration pattern is 2-5 minutes and 4-6 times daily.

(b) Paranoid schizophrenic person are internally more reactive. Therefore, it is also necessary to check their reaction. The graphotherapy for this is –

Fig. 3.1.i.b

It should also be practiced with normal or high speed. This is responsible for normalizing the reactive nature on condition, which would be virtual or real. Practice pattern is 2-5 minutes for 5-10 times a day.

(ii) There are many panic ideas and thoughts come across mind of paranoid schizophrenic person without passing through rational processes are beyond control of person. Such panic thoughts and ideas make person too reactive. Reaction takes place due to conflict between trait of ego and rest of personality. In virtual world, person valuates himself virtually as breaking his correlation with realities according to his own concerns. This is depicted by handwriting many abnormal folds in handwriting owing to disturbance in system of reaction on particular matter or subject on correlation with slow speed of handwriting. Because of paying enough more intention on conditional factors, as considered by person having gap among two words are not regular at somewhere just leaded by occurrence of condition born mental disownity. That permits coming of many unwanted thoughts and later on gap becomes decreased which results abnormal condition born mental overlapping between two successive conditions in real world and virtual world, get prolonged for long time.

Paranoid schizophrenic person does not have trait of self-valuation or not in normal activate form to recognize him. Such trait having person has strong possibilities of coming under grip of paranoid schizophrenia. Therefore, to get rid of such form of this trait or to reform it there is following doodle as graphotherapy –

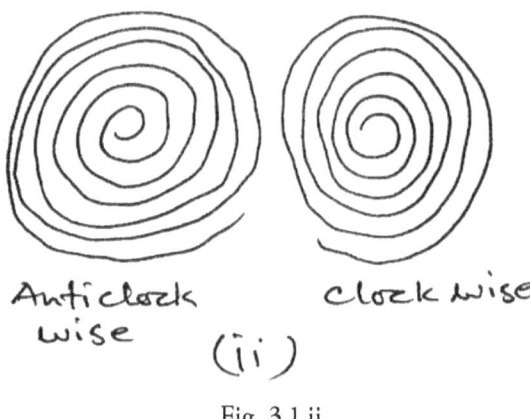

Anticlock wise   clock wise

(ii)

Fig. 3.1.ii

These should be practiced with slow speed for 2-5 minutes 4-6 times a day. Well these all stand for deep self-valuation on the base of happened events or incidents in past.

At the same time the person should have to stand in front of mirror (in which he can see his full image) to self-watch for some long time (for 45 minutes to 1.00 hrs) at least twice a day.

(iii)   It is observed that paranoid schizophrenic person is highly sensitive towards conditions from where virtual worlds could turn into highly active and panic form. The real conditions already have correlated with panic virtual world and status produced by panic thoughts comes directly from continuous hurting ego attached with his secured status. The phenomenon then leads person to be reactive. The thoughts come across mind in the form of panic sound and reaction of person is in same mode i.e. in sound form paranoid schizophrenic persons are produced by negative matters. There is strong possibilities of increasing more negative forms in virtual worlds to the person which will make person more panic as well as provide way to get virtual subject from realities and gradually that virtual panic system starts dominating real world as on reaching there again and again. The mental status regarding this concern is revealed by handwriting as capital and small letters have least difference in size. Due to not doing effort to dominate virtual world the conditions retaining such system to consider most of conditional factors, make person more reactive. There are many anomalous changes in bends and turns of letters due to continuity of those reaction against virtual thoughts and ideas produced from his virtual world and letters are completed in irregular fashion because same factors and reaction do not repeat themselves.

Such persons must have to possess the strong trait of dominating the condition with management. To reform this trait there is following doodle as a graphotherapy –

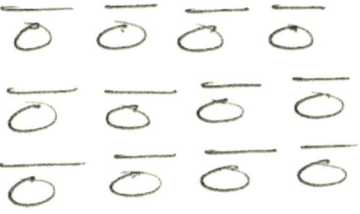

Fig. 3.1.iii

This graphotherapy is to make trait establishment strong with known reasons in known conditions and subject. It should also be practiced with normal speed 2-5 minutes 4-6 times a day.

During that period person must keep him away from serious and horror TV serial episodes, movies, literatures etc.

(iv) Paranoid schizophrenic person always survives as person with factor of willing system is not in proper manner and result is unusual correlations among many fundamental personality traits. The willing system in such person is not in dominating position and that is affected negatively by various external factors, reflect as hallucination. The unfulfilled willing system is observed in handwriting as words are completed carefully as well as being maintained carefully too their trend of furnishing with inappropriate manners. No systematic rhythm is observed in handwriting sample.

Therefore, such person should have to respect their own natural will and must not get more suggestions from others and he must not dependent upon such system. Getting suggestion must be exceptional and rare for him. Regarding this abnormality there is following doodle as graphotherapy –

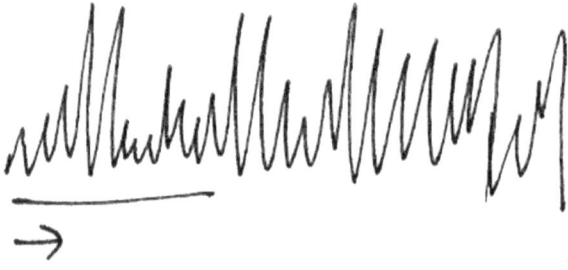

Fig. 3.1.iv

It should be noted here that the elevation of lines should not be same. Breaking in rhythm is not an important matter. It should be practiced with high speed or should be increased gradually. Practice pattern should be of 2-5 minutes 5-10 times a day.

(v)   Paranoid schizophrenic person commonly complaints that he is willing to weep which often comes to him frequently. They always survives in deep grief due to being of dangerous factors across their mind with complete strong system observed in handwriting as occurrence of many sudden breaks owing to improper perception and that results possibilities of getting activated those all dangerous panic conditional factors with strong system. The complete strong systems and its impact lead to form virtual events determine defeat in conflict against reaction. This phenomenon causes persons persistent grief and keeps continuously him in sadness. Another feature of handwriting is in the support of this phenomenon is presence many irregular gap among words. Here the more gaps causes condition born mental disownity responsible for letting many unwanted panic factors come across mind of schizophrenic person and lesser gap causes condition born mental overlapping due to over continuity of hallucination and delusion.

The respect full and pleasurable feeling is must for paranoid schizophrenic person. There is following doodle as graphotherapy –

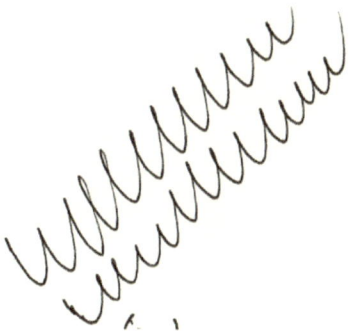

Fig. 3.1.v

This is upward going on 30⁰. The length of elevation must not be less than .5 cm. Normal or more than normal speed is necessary to practice it. It should be practiced 2-5 minutes 2-5 times a day.

(vi) Paranoid schizophrenic person has quite negative attitude about their working on all subjects. Their negative attitude is also one of the important causes of this mental disorder. There are two forms of working of this negative attitude one working easily and lightly on correlation with security system of mind and second is person is compelled for escaping by hard and deep correlation with security system. Escaping works with the form of ego on completing the process of escaping, the subconscious mind of person enquires for further step regarding this concern to be taken. On finding negative answer, it starts to find out his motive of being escaped. As process of finding makes fast the hallucination world from where getting up using most of personality system accordingly. Such "ego-query" is not pleasant process and unacceptable for the person. Then security system of mind becomes activated to bring person in another virtual world just like interrogation with accused person in lock up of police station by police officer. Here ego is police officer, police station and lock up is virtual world and accrued person is rest of fundamental personality traits. The negative attitude is raveled by handwriting as more space taken by down stroke loop, the disturbance in confidence occurred due to negative attitude and process of escaping observed as fluctuation in alignment of handwriting. The interrogations with rest of mind by ego are observed in handwriting, as placements of letters are not in proper and regular manner.

Here there is only need to make person of positive attitude. The following doodle as grophotherapy –

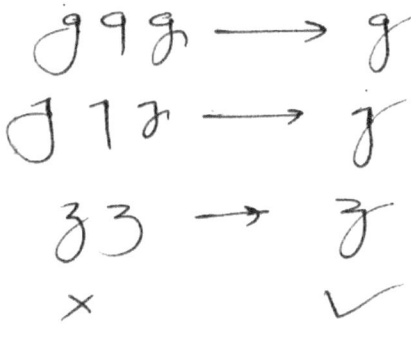

Fig. 3.1.vi

This is not a part of mending but it should be practiced as graphotherapy for 2-5 minutes 5-10 times a day.

(vii) It is found that paranoid schizophrenic person does not have good will towards some particular individuals rather he has bad wills towards them. Such bad wills are in much strong position to deform the natural system of personality. On perception of these factors, the person remains uncreative instantly but person strongly wants to respond them. It starts repeating to damage the trait system by internal reaction. Indeed, the will of such persons are negatively affected by negative and unwanted person born factors yields unusual deformation observed in handwriting as extra care in furnishing the letters, with vibration. Vibration reveals deformed or deforming personality traits due to not expressing himself continuously.

Such person must has to keep good will towards every one if it is in any form those must have to be converted in good will by improving Communication Quotient (Comm.Q.). There is following doodle as a graphotherapy –

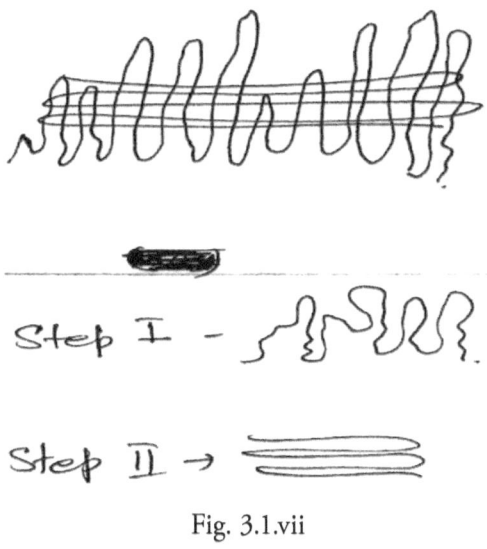

Fig. 3.1.vii

It should be practiced with very slow speed for 2-5 minutes 4-6 times a day.

The graphotherapy stands for developing philosophical trait to control the unusual reactivates. It will also improve the positive "Communication Quotient (Comm. Q.)".

(viii) Paranoid schizophrenic person shows abnormal humbleness against basic instinct. Naturally, they are not humble and have strong will to react but they could not due to being person born factor in much strong position. This is the defeated condition of schizophrenic person by that particular person born strong factor in "battle of social conducts". Starting of this phenomenon is an initial plotting of paranoid schizophrenia. This is recalled in handwriting as there are many abnormal acute folds seen in circular folds because of having will of rigid reaction and the opening and closing of letters are not seen in regular fashion. Most of the situations are undefined and as being of strong negative internal feelings let person leads to deformed letters in irregularly in Handwriting sample.

In such person the trait of humbleness should be increased as much as it could be. To do this there is following doodle as graphotherapy –

They should practice like this way

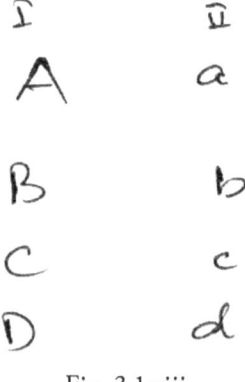

Fig. 3.1.viii

All letters must be closed. This is to increase humbleness in the schizophrenic person. It should be practiced 2-5 minutes 4-6 times a day with slow speed.

(ix) The paranoid schizophrenic person has strong prejudice towards both types one is person born which results of correlation between prejudice and proud and condition and subject born prejudice which is yielded by correlation between conditions and ego. It should be noted that there is no particular symptom of prejudice is observed in handwriting directly. Though some specific furnishing style of letters are reflected at somewhere in handwriting sample but they are not the regular part of rhythm of handwriting. Most of schizophrenic person does not show any rhythm in handwriting that is main feature of having any one of prejudice either person born or subject born. Nevertheless all persons possess both prejudices, which are revealed by slight manic form of handwriting. The objective mainly correlates with proud revealed in handwriting as letters of handwriting are bigger in size (= considering more factors), bad interconnection among them (= no extension of proud and related factors), signature is upward going (= formation of new thoughts), words are tried to well furnished with unsuccessful efforts (= intention on negative approaches of working), abnormal spacing and more than two segmented signature (= disturbed criteria of changing conditions due to person born factors). Bad connectivity of letters, abnormal spacing furnishing of letters and many- segmented signature are observed due to paranoid disorder.

Ego, as a negative trait in paranoid schizophrenic person revealed in handwriting as most of letters are in handwriting are bigger in size in relevant to first capital letter (= because of dominating many conditions and their factors on personality of person on correlating with "high level of comparative establishment of imagination"). Handwriting goes down ward while signature upward going (= due to huge difference between presentation and realities). In handwriting of most of the people, the first letter found bigger (= due to over wean before egoistic effort) and instead of higher speed of signature is signed with very slow speed (= just because of strong intention paid towards availed conditions by their hallucination). Size of letter, alignment of handwriting and signature, speed of handwriting are considerably out of rhythm.

Such person should not have to be prejudice as a negative trait. There is no particular doodle as a graphotherapy to overcome the prejudice. Here it is enough to improve the cerbral activity which covers most of abnormalities regarding prejudice –

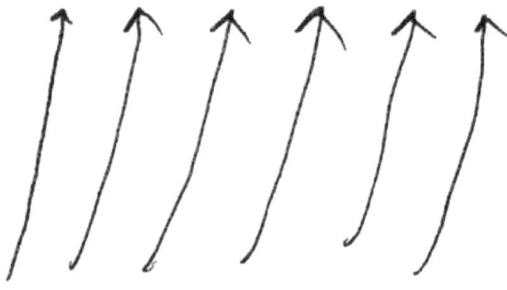

Fig. 3.1.ix

Its elevation must not be less than 1 cm. It should be practiced 2-5 minutes 2-5 times a day with normal speed.

(x)   There are many factors, stimulants are in conditions and circumstances around the schizophrenic person towards which they are highly sensitive against virtual agnation, and all have high possibilities to make person over-reactive. The form of trait revealed in handwriting, as t-bar is place just lower than half due to low enthusiasm and person compel to consider very minute conditional factors for giving reactions. Some people have abnormal loops at starting of sentence and signature. The reason behind this phenomenon is the formation of abnormal eddy current of particular thought getting person prepared for specific strong reaction on particular topic. Latter on that converts into complex and results willing of becoming more cruel regarding giving reactions, speed of handwriting is abnormally slow because of consideration of much factors provided by virtual world and due to which they are not able to pay proper intention on factors provided by real world. At the same time abnormal extra outgrowths are observed in handwriting just because of overreaction.

The condition and circumstances should be favorable for such persons to avoid the overreaction as much as possible. On mental level to avoid many of small stimulants and factor they must have high enthusiasm. To improve it there is following doodle as graphothherapy –

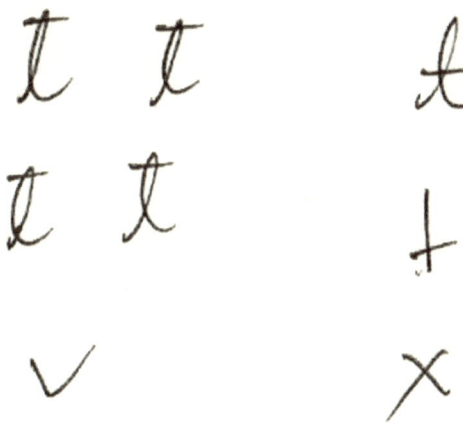

Fig. 3.1.x

Placement of t-bar near the head it should be practiced with slow speed 2-5 minutes 5-10 times a day.

With set of graphotherapies, the person should follow some instructions for better results –

(i)   They must not talk about any one for long time.
(ii)   They should serve any one without expectation or very least or small expectations.
(iii) They must be vegetarian to avoid stimulant of cruelty.
(iv)   They should respond.
(v)   They should have to go to exercises the "Shashkasana" for ensuring proper blood circulation on brain.

UNIT - 4

PERSONALITY DISORDERS

CHAPTER – 1

Personality Disorders

Personality disorder is a general category of mental disorder in which those people are categorized whose mental development so derailed and distorted that their perception & thinking also become maladaptive by rather strong correlations between person and unfavorable conditions in which person has to live or survive. Person becomes enough more agitated. Personality disorder is neither reaction of stress situation nor anxiety. This is a result of improper maturity towards tackling situation and then continuity of personality development get disturbed by doping of various conditional factors forcibly or by compulsion. Symptoms of personality disorder of adolescence are continued to adulthood. Personality disorders are also known as Character Disorders. In fact it is also disorders of distorted personality traits. Carson and Butcher defined is as "personality disorders in general, appears to be extreme or exaggerated pattern of personality trait predispose the individual to troublesome behavior often of are interpersonal nature".

The personality disorder described in DSM-IV as "A personality disorder is enduring patterns of inner experience the exceptions from the culture. Is pervasive and inflexible, has an onset on adolescence or early childhood is stable over time and leads to distress or impairment".

According to DSM-IV (1994) there are 10 types of personality disorder as follows –

1. **Paranoid Personality Disorder** - in paranoid personality disorder, it is found some specific traits like trait of suspicion, hostility, obstinacy etc. are overdeveloped and are expressed in every situation and occasion that results the person repeats often-maladaptive behavior again & again without getting lesson. Therefore, abnormally over consistency in maladaptive behavior of person is observed. Such people are hypersensitive, even they always justify their errors and try to prove themselves always right. Their behavior becomes so tough that are impaired from every point of view. They have hostility of higher rank.

2. **Schizoid personality disorder** - The people of this type of mental disorder have inability to maintain their relationships and they do not have interest towards this side as well. Such person also could not express their emotions properly.

3. **Schizotypal Personality Disorder**- The people of this type of disorder are exclusive, hypersensitive and eccentric in talking. It differs from schizoid disorder in having enough more eccentricity, hypersensitivity, thinking and perception than that of schizoid personality disorder. Such people prominently have knowledge of reality but stereotyped and personal thinking are observed.

4. **Histrionic Personality Disorder** - People of this disorder express such type of behavioral pattern in which immaturity, excitement, emotional imbalance etc. are observe prominently. Commonly their sexual adjustment is also not satisfactory and interpersonal relationships are different and highly drastic. They are highly eager to get approval on every matter from others.

5. **Narcissistic Personality Disorder**- The people of this disorder has abnormally enough stronger superiority complexes. They have strong affection of self-importance, keep themselves on the most important place and suppose other some are mean and lean. They are abnormally highly ambitions and do not let others to come near to them with getting it dependent also. They lack empathy.

EMOTIONAL ENGINEERING | 183

They do not give look disorder into their personality and that results they do not feel need of neither any treatment nor mental empowerment.

6. **Anti-social Personality Disorder** - This is the most common and important type of disorder among all types of personality disorders. Such people ignore society by expressing violence and disruptive behavior.

7. **Avoidant Personality Disorder**- The people of this category is hypersensitive against ignorance of themselves by others. They have limited or very selective social relationships and not interested towards making new relationships and make strong all of those. They have fear of getting self-criticized.

8. **Obsessive-compulsive Personality Disorder**- The people of this category is highly careful against laws, established rituals (not ready for argument) and public recognition according to their own faith, regulation and force matter as that every person should have to freedom to perform himself according to own self. They have disability to express their warm feelings with sense of humor. They are over-inhibited, over conscientious, rigid, obstinate and life full of compulsive orderliness.

9. **Dependent Personality Disorder** - Such type of people are highly dependent on others and whenever they become lonely, feel quite discomfort and lack of confidence instead of being full and complete skill they feel helpless.

10. **Borderline Personality Disorder**- Persons having this disorder have some symptoms of other disorders, which are found effectively along with personality disorder. Beside behavioral problem, "mood shift" is also observed in such people. Even on getting very minute stimulant, the person becomes highly evident. Nature of such person is impulsive and behavior unpredictable, unstable and aggressive.

Symptoms revealed in handwriting - For better identification it needs the handwriting sample of about ½ a page. The symptoms of personality disorders are observed in trace. There are least differences among them –

1. **Paranoid personality disorder**- The people suffering from paranoid personality disorder show d-stem in handwriting, signature or in both with abnormal loop formation in handwriting reveals indication of obstructions due to unfavorable conditions may be in any process towards achieving the goal or contemporary targets. This is actually the matter of perception and upward going signature causes person highly sensitive about their goal related obstructions.

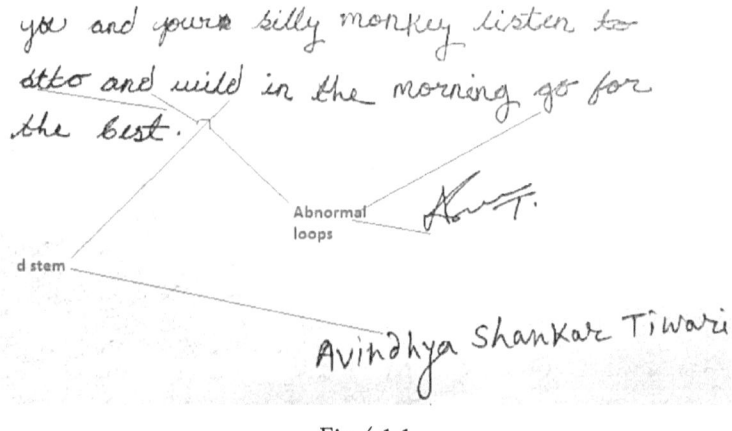

Fig.4.1.1

2. **Schizoid personality disorder** - Such people has single unit of handwriting with extra outgrowth quite more than that of basic need and tinny handwriting. The extra outgrowth of signature reveals the intention of covering other matters or factors anyhow or by any means which could be prolonged for long time. As there matters concern, they are created contemporarily. The tinny handwriting reveals the self-centered personality of the person.

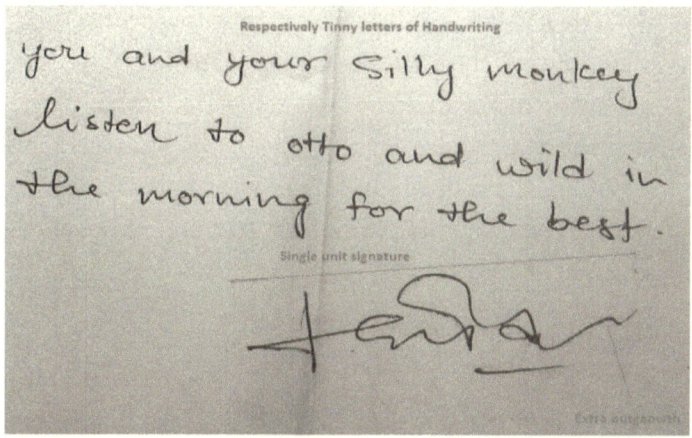

Fig. 4.1.2

3. **Schyzotypal personality disorder** - such person have high elevation in letters due to hypersensitivity, extra long Y- stroke because of possessing exclusive nature, loop born by 's' in its lower portion which recalls the extra responsibility feeling cause eccentricity in talking. Some people also have extra wider letters in handwriting. The fact revealed the consideration of such amount of factors due to which mental abnormality takes place.

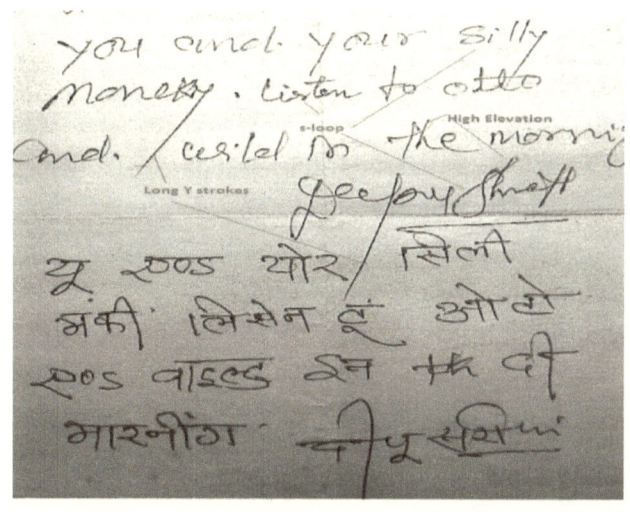

Fig. 4.1.3

4. **Histrionic Personality Disorder** - The people with this disorder have low or very slow speed of handwriting due to being paid extra intention in any matter or subject and not being homogeneous loop at appropriate place. At the same time, some people show amount of additional acute folds in handwriting because of light obstinacy, which is the symptom of immaturity in nature.

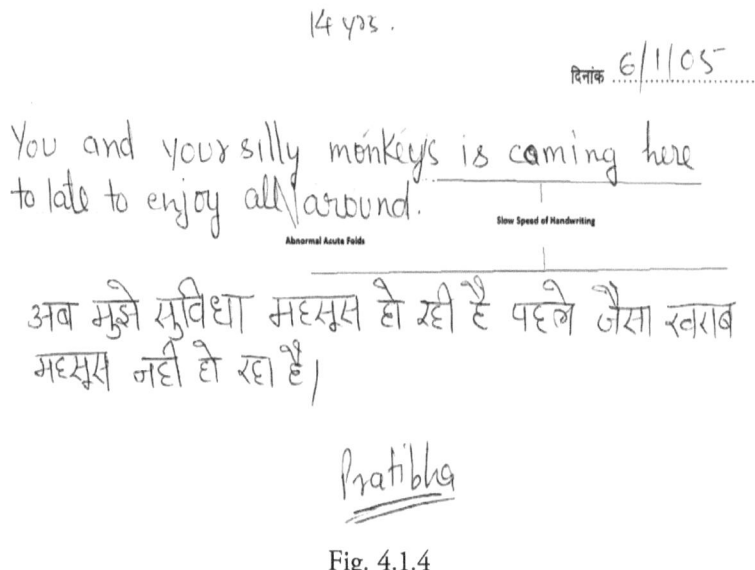

Fig. 4.1.4

5. **Narcissistic Personality Disorder** - Such people make bigger loop in upper part of letter depicts the seeking tendency of factor of high level and effort to establish him in particular or all conditions. That circle covers most of letters or complete letter. Such people also have very slow speed of handwriting because paying more intention on factors conserving their superiority completely correlated with their ego that eagerly demands their own satisfaction.

Loop Covers many part of signature

Fig. 4.1.5.i

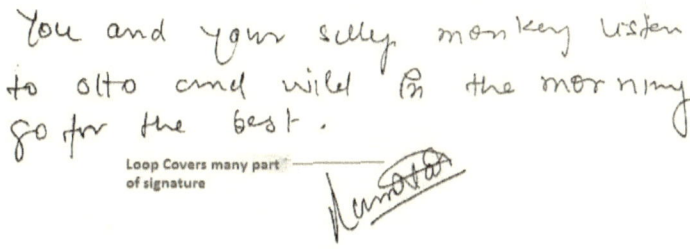

Loop Covers many part of signature

Fig. 4.1.5.ii

6. **Antisocial Personality Disorder**- Such person show blunt end of 't' which depicts the extreme violation of person, high elevation of letters due to having more mental activity towards their activeness. On becoming violent, such people use their extreme mental capacity. At the same time, some of them lack d-loop in both handwriting and signature.

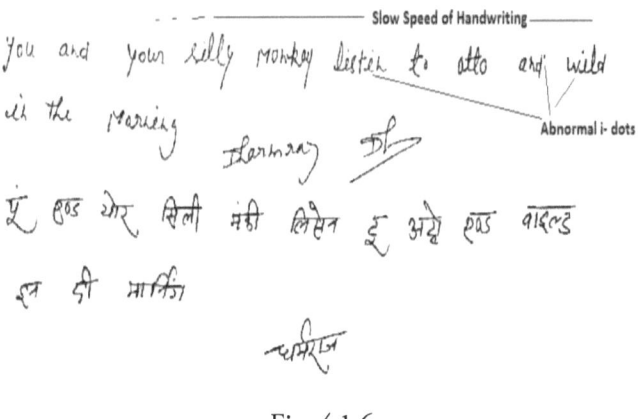

Fig. 4.1.6

7. **Avoident Personality Disorder** - Due to strong self-centered personality, such people have tinny handwriting and controversially the slow speed of handwriting, seen in handwriting sample as well. Whereas having intention to keep high speed of handwriting but could not get succeeded during writing and at somewhere in handwriting sample, deformed i-dots are observed because of abnormal high expectations kept by the persons from the conditions and person born factors.

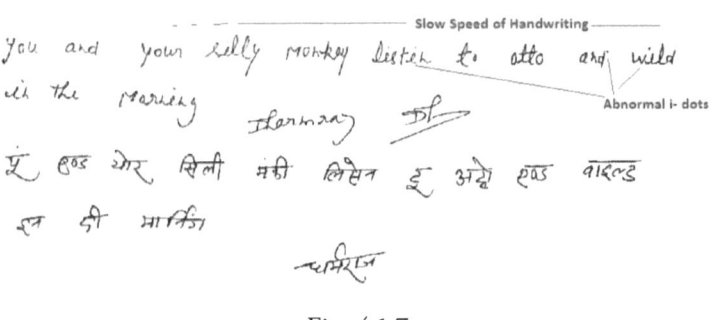

Fig. 4.1.7

8. **Obsessive compulsive personality Disorder** – As OCD in previous unit

9. **Dependent personality Disorder** – Style of handwriting between matching observed in their name and signature, which is completely

inspired and motivated. Abnormally, the rhythm of handwriting is observed unbroken. At some placed consistency of letters seen hardly made.

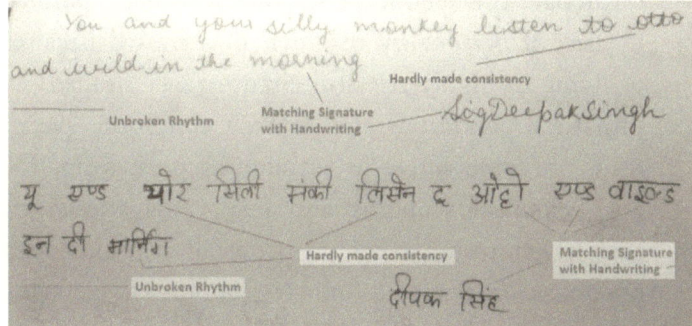

Fig. 4.1.9

10. **Borderline Personality Disorder** – Symptoms of this disorder are not in observed in specific pattern so, therapy should be given as per requirement of personality as in therapeutic Handwriting Analysis Research Report.

Common symptoms among all personality Disorder-

People of all personality disorders have some common symptoms-

i.   All do not have artistic approach
ii.   All maintain over confidentiality or secrets
iii. No ability for analysis
iv.   Poor expressiveness
v.   Poor sociality
vi.   Having rather more hopes or expectations from conditions and persons
vii. Irrelevant happiness

A. **Important Instruction Regarding Making Report -**

Towards reforming personality traits through intrapersonal communication neural pathways of those via brain learning, personality research report is required as mentioned earlier and to prepare therapeutic personality research report. Unlike others in case of personality disorder, it is caused because of working or living in highly stressful circumstance, leaded by adverse and unnatural conditions and in such condition "peak navigational traits" become active in extreme or peak form. On that stage, both external stimulus and peak navigational traits support each other towards dealing external stimulus specifically. The phenomenon leads to showing abnormal behavior because of taking place of distortion in neural pathways of personality traits. Towards maintaining unnatural performance due to distortion in highly stressful and unwanted conditions person compels to consider alike factors. In fact, personality-ridden person fails to distinguish difference between his neutral and unnatural behavior/performance because of disintegration of intelligence. Gradually peak navigational traits start covering whole personality instead of being fundamental personality traits in base. The whole phenomenon is termed as "Navigated Personality Transformation". This is the basic feature of all personality disorders. The "Navigated Personality Transformation" is virtual personality purport to keep close eyes from all stressful causes, unwanted conditional factors and other external stimulus that is in fact checked intrapersonal communication with circumstances. Since fundamental personality traits produce huge number of navigational traits to deal external stimulus so, disorder-ridden person always found him stuck with all stressful factors and therefore, personality of person is made intricate by all time reaction raising strong peak navigational traits rather than fundamental personality traits. Understanding "Emotional Mechanism" through therapeutic personality research report, it will be must to bring making of peak navigational trait under limit according to the personality. Because of using fundamental personality traits feeble then there will be quite different therapeutic personality report as per responses being given by peak navigational traits to external stimulus produced by fundamental personality traits.

1. Improvement is required on creativity in any field like music, art or in literature. Because such person does absolutely not have artistic nature for better extension of his mental dimension. This is revealed by handwriting as –

   (i)   Handwriting is not in manic form.
   (ii) More pressure imposed on paper due to pen.
   (iii) Less than normal speed of handwriting.

2. Such person should be more talkative and should not be more selective on this matter. Because person has some secrets and lack of complete open mind. The trait is depicted by handwriting as –

   (i)   Letters of words are observed in different levels and in irregular form.
   (ii) All letters are completed in anyhow with their accessories.
   (iii) Gap among two successive words are less than normal.
   (iv) Little bit of vibration is observed in handwriting.

3. Such person should avoid making unnecessary confidentiality except very serious matters. Because normally such person are very introvert and they have problem in communication with others that fact leads them formation of improper accountability which is depicted by handwriting as –

   (i)   To balance the loop stroke is made rarely (at only on place in handwriting sample).
   (ii) Bigger letters are made like capital letter.
   (iii) Immature signature (hardly signed completely).

4. 4. As far as possible, such person should express himself or herself maximum. Because person is socially expressive as well as active generally. Trait is revealed by handwriting as –

   (i) The process of completing letters with words does not have uniformity.
   (ii) Letters are in manic form.
   (iii) Immature signature.

5. Such person must have reason of every event happened around them. Even if they are wrong, no matter. Because such people do not have proper curiosity, revealed by handwriting as –

   (i) Light back stroke observed in signature.
   (ii) All strokes are single.
   (iii) Abnormal initials.

6. Such people should avoid having unnecessary hopes from any one. Because such people do not have proper reason of hoping or expectations and no condition are around them regarding same in strong form. This revealed by handwriting as –

   (i) Dot accessories are in circular form.
   (ii) T-bar placed on half.
   (iii) Partial efforts made to decorate the letters.

B. **Graphotherapies** - Therefore, there are graphotherapies may be common for all personality disorders ridden people having base of unique personality features and demands accordingly towards mental empowerment and curing -

(i) Person with personality disorder does not have proper possibilities of using his mental ability towards creativity using those points of views, which are formed contemporarily by the conditions and situations. Such person does not have artistic or creative nature for using better mental abilities. The trait revealed by handwriting as handwriting is not in manic form at any place due to lack of creativity and either less than normal speed of handwriting due to paying more intention on contemporary conditional factors or very quite high speed of same due to not paying proper intentions on condition and their related factors. That is why person does not have interest in music, fine arts, literature or witting or in any other creative works. There is need to improve the interest in any of field. There is following doodle as graphotherapy for this –

Fig. 4.i

These should be highly saluted right ward and practice pattern 2-5 minutes 5-10 times a day with normal speed.

(ii) Such people cannot be open minded but stereotyped. They maintain quite more secrets about themselves rather than normal people and have agitating problems on making themselves open. The traits depicted in handwriting as some letters in handwriting are observed on different level due to discomfort caused by contemporary conditions. All letters are completed carefully with their accessories and closed due to not considering any suitable condition regarding selection of matters on which they could be more talkative, gap among the words are not homogeneous because of having both mental overlapping and disownity cause the person different and temporally interpersonal relationships and likely to be vibration.

Therefore, to overcome this abnormality in trait, there are following graphotherapies –

(a) To reform mental overlapping and disunity the person has to maintain the gap among two words 0.5-1.0 cm.

(b) To make the person more talkative there is following garaphotherapy –

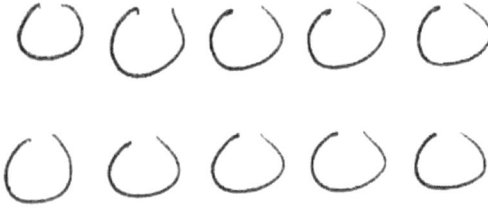

Fig.4. ii.b

There are open circles from upper side. Practice pattern is 2-5 times and 5-10 times daily with slow speed.

(iii)   Person with personality disorder does not have proper curiosity about any subject. Therefore, the possibilities of getting him astonished become feeble. The formation of interest takes place from astonishing point of conditional factors. The deformation of trait revealed in handwriting as slight back-stroke observed in handwriting and signature quiet less than their need due to not running of mentality on partly happened events.

So these people must have to find out the reason of every events concerning with them. There is following doodle as a graphotherapy –

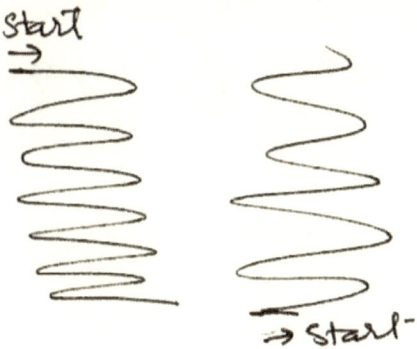

Fig. 4.iii

It should be practiced with slow speed 2-5 minutes 5-10 times a day.

(iv) The people of personality disorder have unnecessary hopes and expectations from the conditions and persons. It is found most of the people do not have proper reason with reasonable justification behind hopes and expectations. Simultaneously, no condition is in such strong position to make more strong hopes from the situation and person born conditions. The trait is revealed in handwriting as dot accessories are deformed i.e. become line or open circle, t-bar placed quiet lower than half due to low enthusiasm of the person and in some letters of handwriting show partial efforts regarding decoration of letters or compilation due deviation in mentality occurs from running condition towards strong establishment of hopes.

There are two doodles as graphotherapies to overcome the unnecessary hopes –

a. To make high enthusiasm the t-bar must place more than half.

Fig. 4.iv.a

b. The i-dot must be in the form of dots and must be marked quite high.

Fig. 4.iv.b

(v) Lack of sociality is common problem in all personality disorder ridden people, which are the most significant. All people face difficulties in management of their sociality and relations. The trait revealed in handwriting as people write erect or slight left slanted due to weaker trait of expressiveness and sociality and lack of laid 'c' in whole handwriting sample.

This person must have strong sociality and expressiveness. There are two doodles as graphotherapies regarding this trait –

a. Firstly, there is much need to increase the confidence to feel social need and then manage all requirements as factors available to the person by society. There is following doodle as graphotherapy –

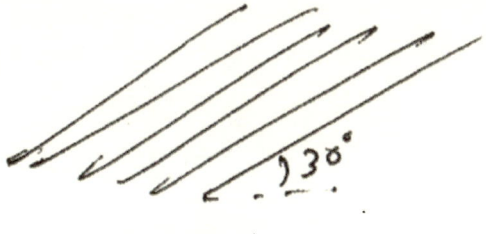

Fig. 4.v.a

These are slanted lines on about 30⁰, should be practiced with high speed 2-5 minutes 4-6 times a day. This is the most suitable to improve confidence for better expressiveness.

b. Second one is to practice laid 'c' or arcade to improve the sociality or if signature is more than one segment then it should be more than one segment.

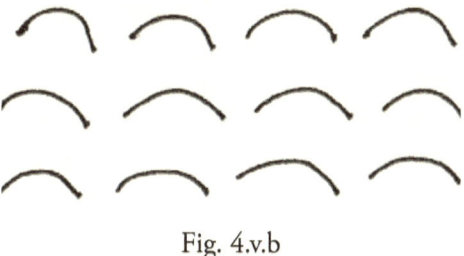

Fig. 4.v.b

It should be practiced with slow speed for 2-5 minutes 5-10 times a day.

(vi) The responsibility feeling in all personality disorder people is observed not in good form. This is because of being strong form superiority trait, obstinacy, and hostility etc. According to the time, the person becomes dependent on those conditional factors, which are the major causes of maladaptive behavior of person. Therefore, there is consistency in maladaptive behavior found in personality disorder person. The lack of responsibility feelings is reeled in handwriting as absence of loop in lower part of 's' and 'S'.

To improve the responsibility feeling in personality disorder person there is following doodle as graphotherapy –

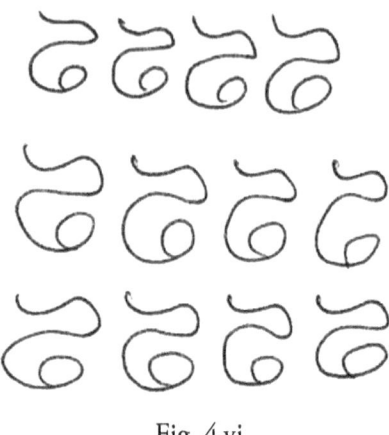

Fig. 4.vi

It should be practiced with slow speed for 2-5 minutes 4-6 times a day.

(vii) Intelligence and happiness are also important traits, which are also observed not in good form of personality-disordered people because of being happiness as result of intelligence. It is necessary to be in good form. The distorted trait of intelligence and as lack of uphill slants and due to lack rhythm of intelligence is observed in distorted form in handwriting sample. Due to breaking rhythm, most of letters are seen in isolated form.

To improve the intelligence and happiness there is following doodle as a graphotherapy –

Fig. 4.vii

There a point to be noted that the elevation of doodle must not be less than 1.0 cm. with little bit of loop should be made with its elevation. The practice pattern is 2-5 minutes 4-6 times a day.

UNIT - 5

DISSOCIATIVE DISORDER

CHAPTER – 1

Dissociative Disorder

Dissociative disorder is a important and very common in which person gets dissociated with his some sort of specific memories integrated to conscious mind and specific mental processes. Some specific parts of memories make specially their own system apart from the person's personality. That may be either in form of different personality or behavior. The dissociative-ridden person responds quite differently his conditions and circumstances. Dissociation is an important matter may be either positive or negative. In positive dissociation, person may be able to direct use most of power of subconscious mind, which is more than 2000 times powerful than subconscious mind according to assumption on comparative shape and size conscious and subconscious minds of Sigmund Freud. Power means every type of ability may be referred as "Supernatural".

Here we will discuss the negative dissociation, which is referred as "Dissociative Disorder". In addition to many things, there are 5 types of major and significant experiences of dissociative disorders –

(i) **Amensia** – People categorized in this section who are not able to recall his memories of prior experiences partially or completely.

(ii) **Depersonalization** – When the person feels detached himself from his general circumstances. He finds himself apart from mainstream of routine life and experiences as flowing with other unnatural and different stream.

(iii) **Derealization** - Person feels whole circumstance as unreal and unbelievable. Therefore, he expects unexpected results and outputs from systems of circumstances.

(iv) **Identity Alteration** – Sometimes person found himself with some special surprising skill. Such skill actually exists in him but person is quite unaware with that. Whenever, answered ability comes in practice even for short time, person get surprised. It may be in infinite form such as finding out any device, technique, discoveries, speeches, foreign words, special information, mode of presentation etc.

Types of Dissociative Disorder

There are four major types of dissociative disorders –

1. Dissociative Amensia
2. Dissociative Fugue
3. Dissociative Identity Disorder (DID)
4. Depersonalization Disorder

1. **Dissociative Amensia** - The behavioral form of such person causes to produce stress because of not recalling his complete experiences or even partially. The cause may be due to mental trauma. This phenomenon leads person to bad sociality, misdeed, adjustment problem and many problems. There are many types amnesia –

(i) **Retrograde Amensia** - This is just localized amnesia, which causes or have caused mental trauma. Person wants to forget all past traumatic memories just before of trauma mishap occurred on that particular place.

(ii) **Post-traumatic Amensia** – This is categorized as when a person is not able to recall experiences of events after trauma and related concerns as well.

(iii) **Anterograde Amensia** – Person fails in recalling new experiences.

(iv) **Selective or Categorical Amensia** – When person recalls some selective information regarding particular category rather than whole.

(v) **Generalized Amensia** – Throughout life, person fails to recall whole experiences of his life.

(vi) **Continuous Amensia** – In this category person can recall some particular experiences rather than whole.

(vii) **Systematized Amensia** – When a person is unable to recall his even specific experiences regarding particular events with information directly related to him.

Out of these seven, any one is if showing symptoms of generalized ameneia, continuous amensia and systematized amensia, will be categorized under dissociative disorder. Such person is treated as serious patients. It may be occurred in any age group either in any child or in old man including adults (male and female both). Duration of amensia undetermined and indefinite means it may be anything from seconds to many years.

2. **Dissociative Fugue** – Person suffering from this disorder get transformed into just other personality having new identity. Person forgets his original identity throughout. At the same time with transformation, the symptoms of amensia are also observed as well. It is often seen that such type of person goes long way from his native or home area and starts new life with new identity and they continue their new identity for many-many years. Suddenly someday, his get surprised on finding himself in just new place that how did he come here, how and why?

Dissociative disorder takes place after severe mental trauma or shock by which person affected profoundly. After such mishap, person are so immature, self-centered and suggestion expecting regarding every concern that he needs help in every concern.

Whenever such person has to face very unwanted, unfavorable, panic conditions and there is no way to bypass by any mean, there is more chances its attack. Only 0.2% people are suffers from this disorder.

3. **Dissociative Identity Disorder** – Commonly it is also known as "multiple personality disorder". In DID there may be more than one personality within one. Each personality status is far more emotional, well organized and thoughtfully highly sophisticated. Having such properties, each personality has its own thought, point of view and developed cognitive system. After spending some time (maybe some weeks, months or years), person either comes back in his own personality or gets transformed into other personality. Each personality is quite different from other one. If in one personality person is too funny, joyful, stress-less then it may be that he is too serious, stress-full, calm in other personality. It was observed that sometimes there are differences of gender occurred in same personality and even no more among different personalities. Each and every personality has is its own different identity that is why it is called "Dissociative Identity Disorder".

Symptoms revealed by Handwriting – There are following symptoms revealed by handwriting through which dissociative disorder-redden person can be diagnosed –

(i) The words of handwriting are abnormally dissociated. This rule may be followed by letters also. This is just because of dissociation of person from his own and original personality system. The rhythm of life is not in its routine, the dissociation of letters or words as depicted in handwriting sample. After dissociation, words and letters are bound to correlate with other emotional system. Person is bound to recall many of panic and unwanted experiences that cause break or dissociation in handwriting sample.

(ii)   Abnormal deformations in many letters are significant feature of this abnormality. This is because of arriving such factors in person's emotional systems, which compel person to get another system apart from his original and fundamental that is in fact personality transformation. Indeed, such deformations are a system in its own. Presence of deformation is just like to make person too usual to get into prospective format. There is nothing in person's own psycho system except panic experiences at particular time person feels like such. Deformed letters obviously a system for fugue for an instance or for long time.

(iii) Some letters excepting uppercase are seen abnormally tinny sized in comparison to others because of being person self-centered in handwriting. However, in the person the damaged ego still exists in the personality of dissociative disorder person but fails to leave positive impact on personality in such people on correlating other personality traits. Thus, it results insisting person to go on other format of virtual personality, which was remaining suppressed. Rather big differences between size of upper and lower case letters create space for shaping other psycho-systems on correlating with other factors, which may be either missing or recalling in positive or negative way.

(iv)   Dissociative disorder-ridden people show blunt end "t", "d" in handwriting. This is the feature of common occurrence because of coming violent reaction when whole factors are missing while demand. The phenomenon leads to insist person to be over violent reaction on any matter. The form of reaction may be change person to person, according to problems what he had to face, and as solution, what he has. As on fugue attack, there may be a sudden change in form of reaction. In fact, the alteration of personality is just a peak form violent reaction i.e. because of "fight or flight" theory. Well, this is applicable in endocrinology but here it is also applicable.

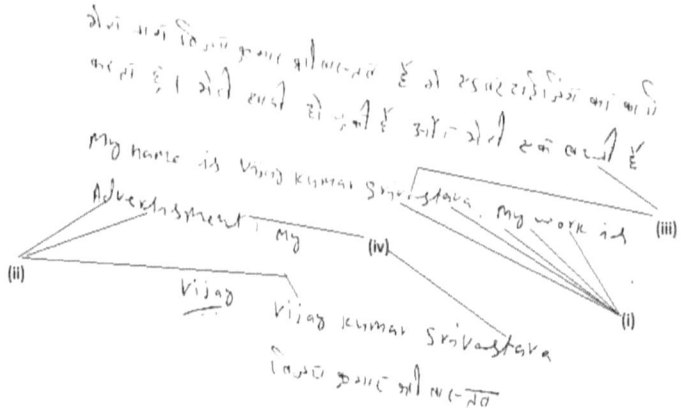

Fig. 5.1.1

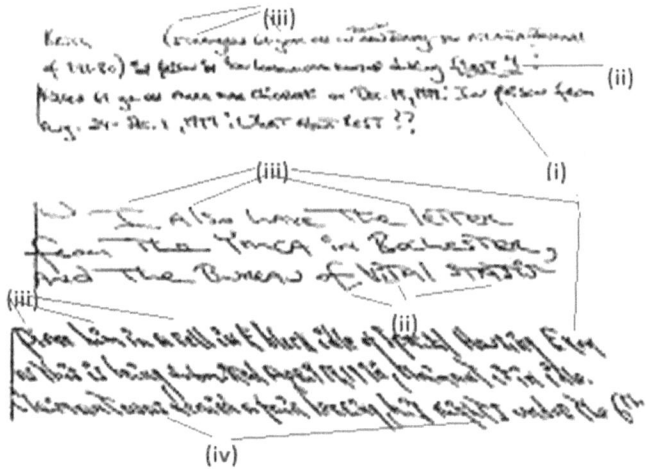

Fig. 5.1.2

A. Important Instruction Regarding Making Report -

Towards reforming personality traits through intrapersonal communication neural pathways of those via brain learning, personality research report is required as mentioned earlier and to prepare therapeutic personality research report. Unlike others in case of dissociative disorder is caused because of working or living in highly anxious circumstance, leaded by mental trauma and in such condition "peak navigational traits" become active in extreme or peak form. On this stage, both external stimulus and peak navigational traits support each other towards dealing external stimulus specifically. The phenomenon leads to showing abnormal behavior because of taking place of distortion in neural pathways of personality traits. Towards maintaining unnatural performance due to distortion in highly stressful and unwanted conditions person compels not to consider unlike factors. In fact, dissociative disorder-ridden person had better distinguish difference between his neutral and unnatural conditional factors caused him trauma and leads to severe anxiety because of focused distorted intelligence. Gradually peak navigational traits start creating new personality system keeping apart all factors causing him severe anxiety, still of being some important fundamental personality traits in base. The whole phenomenon is termed as "Placatory Personality Transformation". This is the basic feature of all personality disorders. The "Placatory Personality Transformation" is virtual personality purport to keep close eyes from all anxious causes, unwanted conditional factors and other external stimuli. Since fundamental personality traits produce number of navigational traits to deal external stimulus so, dissociative disorder-ridden person always found him stucked with all anxious factors and therefore, personality of person is made intricate by all time reaction giving strong peak navigational traits on correlation with some fundamental personality traits. Understanding "Emotional Mechanism" through therapeutic personality research report, it will be must to bring under limit formation of peak navigational traits according to the personality. Because of strong use of some significant personality traits. There will be quite different therapeutic personality report as per unique form of mental trauma being given by peak navigational traits to external stimulus produced by fundamental personality traits.

B. **Graphotherapies** – There are following doodle as graphotherapies towards curing dissociative disorder. This must be given to the person as per demand of personality and what revealed by handwriting –

(i) Firstly, there is much need to increase the confidence to feel social need and then manage all requirements as factors available to the person by society. There is following doodle as graphotherapy –

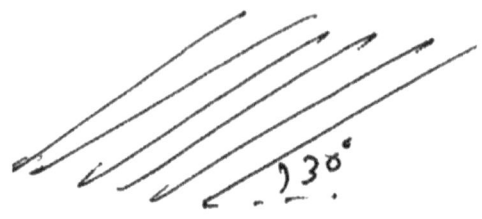

Fig. 5.1.i

These are slanted lines on about 30⁰, should be practiced with high speed 2-5 minutes 4-6 times a day. This is the most suitable to improve confidence for better expressiveness.

(ii) Intelligence and happiness are also important traits, which are also observed not in good form of personality-disordered people because of being happiness as result of intelligence. It is necessary to be in good form. The distorted trait of intelligence and as lack of uphill slants and due to lack rhythm of intelligence which is observed in distorted form in handwriting sample. Due to breaking rhythm, most of letters are seen in isolated form.

To improve the intelligence and happiness there is following doodle as a graphotherapy –

Fig. 5.1.ii

There is a point to be noted that the elevation of doodle must not be less than 1.0 cm. with little bit of loop should be made with its elevation. The practice pattern is 2-5 minutes 4-6 times a day.

(iii) The people of personality disorder have quiet unnecessary hopes and expectations from the conditions and persons. It is found many of those people do not have proper reason behind hopes and expectations what they have. At the same time, no condition is observed in such strong position to make it more strong hopes from the situation and person born conditions. The trait is revealed in handwriting as dot accessories are deformed i.e. become line or open circle, t-bar placed quiet lower than half due to low enthusiasm of the person and in some letters of handwriting show partial efforts regarding decoration of letters or compilation due deviation in mentality occurs from running condition towards strong establishment of hopes.

There are two doodles as graphotherapies to overcome the unnecessary hopes –

    c. To make high enthusiasm the t-bar must place more than half.

Fig. 5.1.iii.a

d. The i-dot must be in the form of dots and must be marked quite high.

Fig. 5.1.iii.b

(iv)   Dissociative disorder-ridden person shows their abnormal reaction against their basic instant. Naturally, they are not like what they are showing as reaction and have strong will to react but they could not due to being person born factor in much strong position. This is the defeated condition of such people by that particular person born strong factor in "battle of social conducts" like some person paranoid schizophrenia. This is recalled in handwriting as there are many abnormal acute folds seen in circular folds due to having will of rigid reaction and the opening and closing of letters are not seen in regular fashion. That is just due to being of strong negative internal feelings, that is undefined situation and expressiveness sub continuously.

In such person the trait of humbleness with proud should be increased as much as it could be. To do this there is following doodle as graphotherapy –

They should practice like this way

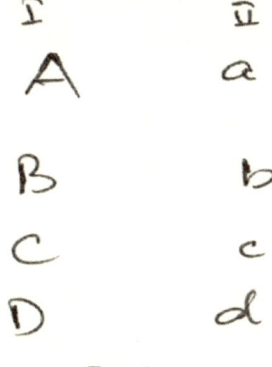

Fig. 5.1.iv

All letters must be closed. This is to increase humbleness in the schizophrenic person. It should be practiced 2-5 minutes 4-6 times a day with slow speed.

(v)   Dissociative disorder-ridden person has quite negative attitude about their working on all subjects. Their negative attitude is also one of the important causes of this mental disorder. There are two forms of working of this negative attitude one works with easy and light correlates with security system of mind and second is to person is compelled for escaping by hard and deep correlation with security system. Escaping tendency works with the form of ego and on completing the process of escape the subconscious mind of person enquires for further step regarding this to be taken. On finding negative answer, it starts to find out his motive of getting escaped. As process of finding makes fast the amnesia and new world from where getting up using most of personality system accordingly. Like paranoid schizophrenia, dissociative disorder person also go through such "ego-query", which is not pleasant process and unacceptable for the person and then the security system of mind becomes activated to bring person in another virtual world just like interrogation with accused person in lock up of police station by police man. Here ego is police man which is in damaged form, police station and lock up is virtual world and accrued person is rest of fundamental personality traits. The negative attitude is raveled by handwriting as more space taken by down stroke loop, the disturbance in confidence due to negative attitude and process of escaping observed as fluctuation in alignment of handwriting. The interrogations with rest of mind by ego seen in handwriting placement of letters are not in proper and regular manner.

Here there is only need to make person of positive attitude. The following doodle as grophotherapy –

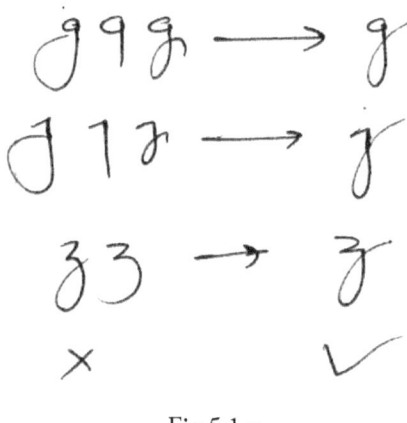

Fig.5.1.v

This is not a part of mending but it should be practiced as graphotherapy for 2-5 minutes 4-6 times a day.

(vi)   There are least factors of happiness with thoughtfulness available to such person. Happiness plays important role in overcoming the emotional anxiety in dissociative disorder person. Such person pays quite more intimation on their contemporary target or objectives occur until anxiety stress and these people also have high curiously about coming condition due to which they become much emotionally stressed along. This is depicted by handwriting as presence of many sudden breaks in handwriting sample. It is needed to make them happy by creating new trait. The made of perception must not serious.

There is following doodle to create the trait of happiness as graphotherapy here one fact should be kept in mind that making of loop is very important-

Fig.5.1.vi

This is should be practiced with normal speed for 2-5 minutes and 4-6 times a day.

(vii)   Person should use normal conditional factors for communication because logic power does not sustain for long time as having irregular speed of handwriting. The symptom is characterized by normal speed of handwriting, letters of handwriting do not found in homogeneous fashion and gap among words is seen in irregular fashion, which is observed more than normal and somewhere seen lesser than that of. Due to irregular gap there is conflict occurred between two traits i.e. condition born mental overlapping and mental disownity. Therefore to adapt such trait person must have to go for following changes in his handwriting as –

a.   Person has to slow his handwriting and signature speed.

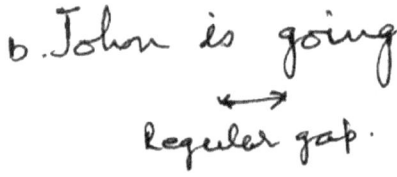

Fig. 5.1.vii.a

b. Gap among towards must be regular.

Fig. 5.1.vii.b

(viii) Person should not go for infinite activation form on any subject or topic. All campaign of various topics and subjects should have impact according to their own format. During continuity, the person should react according to the subjects. This is the process by which, new courses of thought and mode of thinking may come under consideration. The person should stop on particular subject for definite time.

For this purpose person should practice following doodle for 4-6 times a day for 2-5 minutes.

Fig. 5.1.viii

It has to be practiced with slow speed and with intention that it is just more than dot and less than line.

(ix)   In person of dissociative disorder, it is normally found that ambition is not as clear to achieve the particular goal not and at the same time no other ambition like other emotional factors are seen in "saturation stage". It is very necessary for the person to come out of this stage on priority because of being saturation stage as having intention to change mode of perception by change in mechanism of perception with the help of its all related factors are in composite form. Any type of factors would be social, economic, personality or academic related. To come out of this stage, person has to make either new ambition or raise his ambition according to his personality. This is the "inside warded saturation stage" which is characterized in the handwriting as handwriting and signature both are not uniformly upward going. Such phenomenon depicts clearly that no more high ambition observed in the patient that would be more than contemporary status.

The graphotherapies to insure coming out of this saturation stage emotional system due to which person is not able to think better about understandings of related circumstances system to get more conditional factors according to his personal requirements would have to be helpful in emotional thrive of the person -

This is composed of two if two figures one is high speed drown upward lines which should be started from bottom and other one is small circles which should made under the drawn line is perpendicular area from upper side to down and in right side. Circles should make with slow speed.

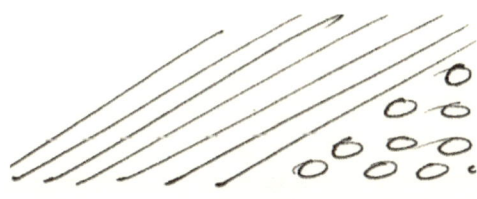

Fig. 5.1.ix

(x)   The dissociative disorder persons have some extra need of exaggeration on any subject in some sort of abnormal way to better sense of his circumstances, situations and related condition. As normally, they are introvert in which condition the intention of exaggeration creates anomaly in his conduct and behavior. Therefore, he starts the efforts to communicate however with responding the results of his exaggerated conducts. In handwriting such symptoms depicted by most of letters of handwriting are closed whereas same letters are open, many of letters are completed anyhow and not in same fashion, signature goes downward first tern upwards slightly and signature has slight vibration.

The exaggeration from of extroversion is an abnormal status. It would beneficial if communication goes on worth fully. This is why the contemporary target will be clear as person expects from situation then goes to consider all related conditional factors along. Therefore, there is only one graphotherapy to overcome the anomaly regarding this trait.

Ist step   -   a draw a circle

IInd step   -   Then draw bar just upper side of circle, it should be

It should be practiced with slow speed for 2 to 5 minutes for 4-6 times daily

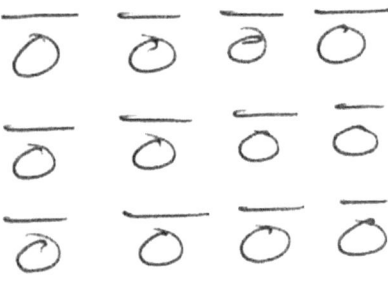

Fig. 5.1.x

(xi) Such persons have strong logic power towards depressive system. The handwriting shows broken rhythm of mental flow which results formation of 'isolated letter' in words.

To maintain the mental flow through rhythm of logic power on various conditional factors, it is necessary to combine letters in rhythmic form.

Such letters have to be into the habit of writing of the depressed person.

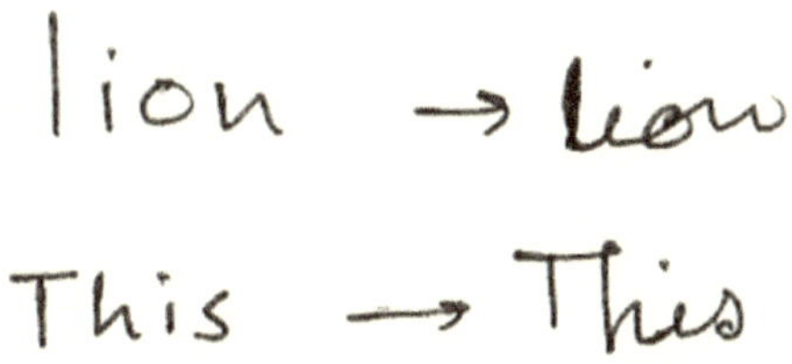

lion → lion

This → This

Fig. 5.1.xi

UNIT - 6

PHYCHOSOMATIC DISORDERS

CHAPTER - 1

Psychosomatic Disorder

Such disorders are categorized as when a person expresses their emotional conflicts, mood disorders, stresses, mental maze and anxiety in the form of actual bodily symptoms. Therefore, there is much real physical disease shown by body by hacking of psychological causes. The significant features of such disorder with symptoms are shown by various organs of body under control of autonomous nervous system like heart, kidney, intestine, skin activities etc.

There are following facts about the nature of psychosomatic disorders –

(i)   There are clear symptoms of somatic diseases in psychosomatic disorder.

(ii)   However, there are somatic disease but the cause are completely psychological. In other words, the causes of such diseases are emotional conflict, anxiety, mental stress, mental maze etc. are significantly observed in stage of psychoneurosis. These diseases are such serious that become chromic where as the causes of psychoneurosis are not.

(iii)   Only those organs, which are under control of autonomous nervous system, get affected. Organs of central nervous system do not affected due to being under direct voluntary control.

(iv)   The suffering person remains unknown about his emotional state consciously.

TYPES OF PSYCHOSOMATIC DISORDER-

According to American Psychiatric Association (APA) there are 10 types of psychosomatic disorders –

1. **Psychophysiological Cardiovascular Disorder** – related to blood vessel.
2. **Psychophysiological Endocrine Disorder** – categorized endocrine diseases.
3. **Psychophysiological Hemic and Lymphatic Disorders** – categorized diseases of lymphatic system.
4. **Psychophysiological Gastrointestinal Disorder** – this is categorized diseases cause to digestive tract.
5. **Psychophysiological Respiratory Disorder** – categorized respiratory diseases.
6. **Psychophysiolagical Genitourinary Disorder** - categorized genitourinary disorder.
7. **Psychophysiological Musculoskeletal Disorder** –. Back ache muscular stress, arthritis etc are kept in this category.
8. **Psychophysiological Organ Of Special Sense** – chromic conjunctivitis are kept in this category.
9. **Psychophysiological Skin Disorder**- neurodermatosis scraching and itching are kept under this category.
10. **Psychosomatic Disorder of Other Types** – such diseases are catagorised in which emotional factors play important role in nervous system.

CHAPTER – 2

Psychophysiology Cardiovascular Disorder

This is a category of blood vessel related disorder caused by mental problems. It includes tachycardia, Anginal syndrome, coronary diseases, headache, migraine etc. This is commonly known that heart is the most sensitive organ against emotional status, so on occurrence of mental problem, the heartbeat become irregular i.e. gets increased by 72 to 150 beats per minutes. Tachycardia may occur any time any time, in any condition or on any place.

SYMPTOMS OF PSYCHO-PHYSIOLOGICAL CARDIOVASCULAR

Disorder in handwriting - There is following symptoms of psychophysiological vascular disorder –

(i)   Psychophysiological cardiovascular disorder ridden person shows some sort of very big letters in handwriting sample at random because of activation of unhealthy ego facing various unfavorable conditions. The unhealthy ego remains laying on steady state but that become enough more active by any or many external stimulants which is quiet uncommon for that particular person. This is common feature of all psychophysiological cardiovascular disorder shown by handwriting.

(ii) The next common feature in handwriting of psychophysiological cardiovascular disorder is the lesser spacing between two words i.e. less than .5 cm. cause condition born mental overlapping. This more clear in mother language (Hindi as I have). Such persons do not get him provided mental rest for proper preparation before forthcoming next condition. The phenomenon results the arising of confusion and perplexing which becomes reason of stress that directly cause psychophysiological cardiovascular disorder in person.

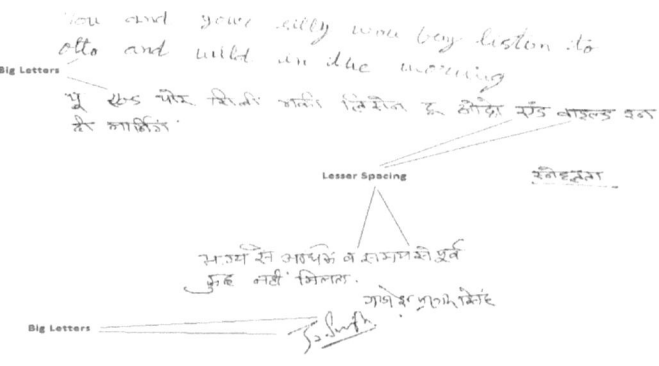

Fig. 6.1

A. Tachycardia –

This is the disorder having irregular heart rhythm and gradual increment in heartbeat. Such person expresses their inner conflict in form of irregular rhythm of heartbeats, weakness and sometime problem in breathing that beat may reach by 75 to 150 beats / minutes. Tachycardia may attack any time and in any condition. According to Kicker- 1994 such persons are highly competitive but have fear of success and fear of remaining unsuccessful in same amount in their competitive lives.

Symptoms of Tachycardia in Handwriting- there are following symptoms shown by handwriting of such person suffering from tachycardia –

(i)   The people who suffer from tachycardia, generally have high enthusiasm but at some place of handwriting, the t-bar is observed less than half which is abnormal, depicts something is going on against his mental status or state of mind and simultaneously become quite sensitive matter for person. On facing such conditions quite unexpected, leads people to disturbances in the heartbeat and the volume.

(ii)   In handwriting of such person, at many places uphill slants are observed reveals person use their mind for deep analysis all unexpected conditions or situations to which he facing off. Because of this, they become highly sensitive about their personal unwanted conditions and their all factors related to them anyway. It is also found the uphill slants make high elevation in relevant letters like l, t, d etc. Such high elevation in letters makes person highly sensitive towards the conditions and situation as well.

(iii)   Most of the person of Tachycardia writes left slanted which reveals cold hearted and socially unexpressive. The problem is due to being them highly competitive in comparison to others.

(iv)   The last significant feature in the person having Tachycardia is controversial conflict in personal expression possessed by person. The features depicted in handwriting as at some places many letter are observed open where as some letters are strictly closed like 0. They do not have proper management of expression. Abnormally both expression and not expression create problem.

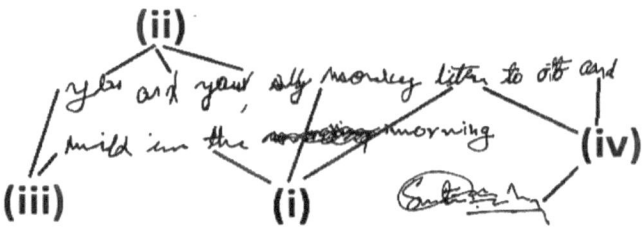

Fig. 6.1.A.1

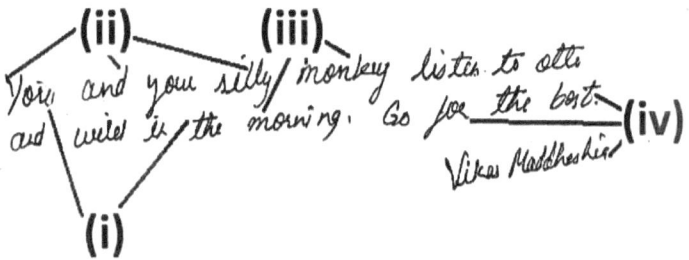

Fig, 6.1.A.2

A. **Important Instruction Regarding Making Report** – In such cases mind uses body for giving reaction to external, internal or both stimuli. On initial stages mind itself give proper reaction and even on level it deals with all stimuli using emotional and security system. However, on being discontent and weakening reaction leads to remain fail in dealing all stimuli, mind starts using body which is termed as "psychosomatic disorders". The concept holds fact that most of physical disorders remain on just psycho level for long duration and after being failed in dealing on that level, those become physical or somatic. The phenomenon felicitates us to diagnose all of those just remaining on very psycho level. "Emotional Engineering" not only diagnoses those all physical disorders on just initial psycho level quite before appearing symptoms in body but also can cure too.

On still remaining unchanged form and properties of stimuli, to give more reaction the fundamental personality traits produce huge number of peak navigational traits to make body physically hyperactive towards vanquishing the effects of stimuli. The phenomenon results most of visceral and other organs start working fast to gain result as soon as possible. If this phenomenon persists in body for long time, becomes psychosomatic disorders. Gradually endocrine system also becomes a part of this activity and using its whole system in giving reaction unnecessarily leads to endocrine disorders. This is all to minimize effects of stimuli which may be either external, internal or both.

Towards curing, the required fundamental personality traits it must be strengthening according to demand of unique personality. Since in such cases huge amount of peak navigational traits are involved according to the stimuli and unique personality, there would be much more variation to be diagnosed by handwriting sample understanding Emotional Mechanism. Therefore, careful attentiveness is needed in preparation of therapeutic personality research report for proper and to the point intrapersonal communication. The instruction will be applicable for all types of psychosomatic and endocrine disorders.

B. **GRAPHOTHERAPIES** - There are following graphotherapies to vanquish the problem of tachycardia due to emotional problems –

(i)   The persons have abnormal form of expressiveness which is revealed in handwriting as many letters are observed in closed form where as some letters are in open form. Well it may be controversial but expressiveness must be in homogeneous from in most of the conditions what type of situation is around person. The person must not maintain unnecessary confidentiality and on any leakage even in little bit, matter becomes enough more sensitive.

There is following doodle as graphotherapy to make person proper expressive and extend this trait homogeneously in over all personality –

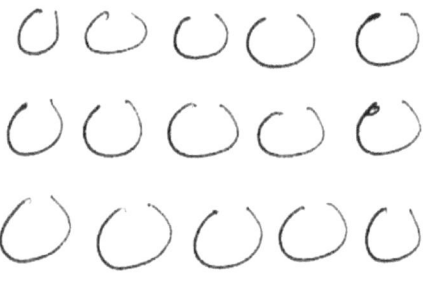

Fig.6.1.i

This is open 'o' from upper side. The elevation of letter must be appropriate. The practice pattern should be 2-5 minutes 5-10 times a day.

(ii) Person suffering from Tachycardia must not be over reactive, should be almost homogeneous and have definite pattern of giving reaction in all conditions and circumstances. Therefore, it is very necessary to overcome the hyperactivity. There is following doodle as graphotherapy.

Fig. 6.1.ii

These are small straight lines, which should be practiced with slow speed, and gap among two lines should be almost homogeneous. After 7 days of practice speed of practice should increase gradually. The pattern of duration 2-5 is minutes 5-10 times a day.

(iii) People suffering from tachycardia are also highly sensitive towards their matter of ego. They have very limited subjects for consideration to extend their mental activities. Due to being this limitation of mental activity, there are high possibilities of becoming person more reactive within the limits. To overcome this problem the philosophical traits are very useful for proper mental extension and keep person away from unnecessary reaction. It is also observed that such persons have more eagerness towards considering subject and tackling those as per ego accordingly. This is the major problem. There is following doodle as graphotherapy for creating philosophical trait in the person –

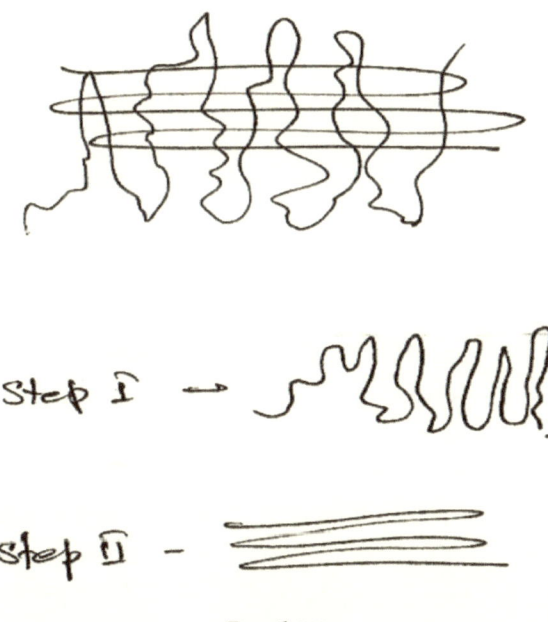

Fig. 6.1.iii

In second step doodle must be upward going. The whole doodle should be practiced with slow speed and should complicate within 2-5 min. 5-10 times a day.

(iv)   In handwriting of such people, there are many uphill slants are occurred at some places because of intermittent high intelligent mental activities on some particular subjects. Uphill slants are not observed homogeneously and in uniform fashion. The phenomenon depicts the selective activeness for selective activities for more perception to extreme respond using maximum intelligence. This is not normal perception. This is more than normal revealed by their elevation.

It is necessary for such person to make it normal with high activeness. There is following doodle as graphotherapy –

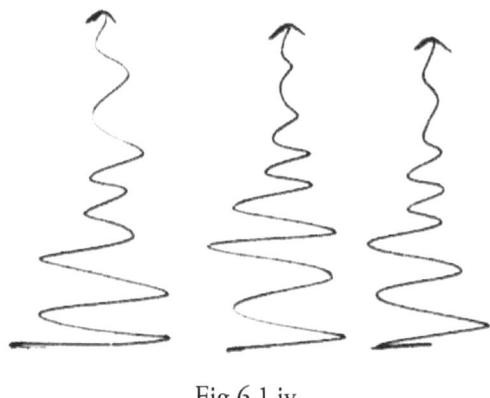

Fig.6.1.iv

It should be practiced with high speed as much as possible. This stands for performing high mental activeness perception mostly available conditional factors. The practice pattern should be 2-5 minutes for 5-10 times a day.

(v)   Artistic or creative approach is also quite helpful to overcome the psychosis of tachycardia. Such person does not have proper possibilities of mental ability for creative using those points of views, which arise contemporarily from situations and intellectual senses. Person also does not have artistic nature for using mental ability in better creative way. The trait revealed by handwriting as the handwriting is seen in manic form at any place. The creativity is necessary to make them deviate from such factors on which the person becomes more reactive. Slow speed of handwriting depicts the person paying quite more intention on contemporary unfavorable condition due to which person is compelled for becoming more reactive that directly affects the heart beat.

Such person do not has any intention in art, music, and writing and in any creative work. It is necessary to develop the interest in creativities-artistic approaches there is following doodle as graphotherapy-

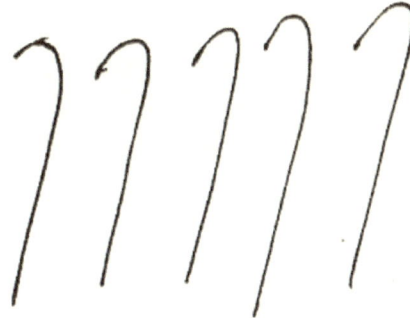

Fig. 6.1.v

This is slanted curved lines should be practiced with normal speed for 2-5 minutes 4-6 times a day.

(vi) The last graphotherapy is to keep in mind that it must be given proper spacing among the words to keep person away from mental overlapping. Such person should give proper time to their mind for next condition, which is important to keep under proper consideration. In this phase, mind imagines and make proper layout about coming condition. Therefore, gap between two words must not be less than 0.5 cm.

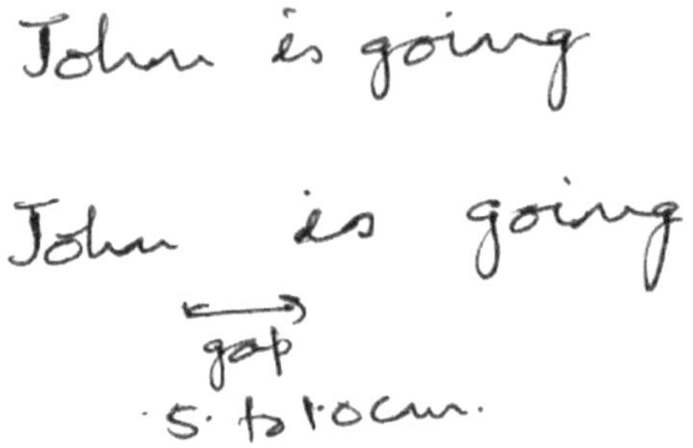

Fig. 6.1.iv

C. Coronary Diseases

There are huge numbers of people died of this disease. This is also a common disorder of cardio-vascular disorder in which blood clots in those arteries, that supplies blood to the heart results heart attack. Because of occurring this phenomenon, there is considerably loss of tissues of heart and becomes distorted. However, it has physiological cause but emotional stress plays very important role. Hence, through controlling emotional stress it can be avoided up to a great extent. According to Freedman & Risenman "a person of type A has more possibilities of coronary disorder". On psycho level, all stress causing factors may cause this disorder like being highly ambitious, having strong competition with your close ones, perplexing mind, mental maze etc. As symptoms, all are revealed by handwriting as upward going signature high, underline owing to having high ambition, fluctuation in alignment of sentence due to having perplexing mind lead to cause another symptom, which is observed as well i.e. lesser spacing among words. At somewhere, it becomes abnormal overlapping for long time and then sudden mental disownity having high sensitivity, the handwriting shows some abnormal vibration. The abnormality is obvious prominently in circular folds.

According to Kroger "the cardiac muscle become excited and peripheral resistance become increased both decrease the clotting time". According to Jones (1982) "there is positive correlation between emotional stress and clotting time". Those people who has chronic emotional stress has high possibility of get into grip of coronary disease.

GRAPHOTHERAPIES- to overcome the emotional stress there is following doodles as a graphotherapies –

(i)   There is quite lesser spacing between two words i.e. less than 0.5 cm, which is due to paying more intention on their contemporary targets or objectives. Such targets and objectives are the main cause of stress. Due to condition born mental overlapping person come in quite hurry to achieve all targets, objectives and even goal. In most of the cases, the efforts of achieving objective or target directly correlate with person's ego and then is becomes main issue having attraction.

So as a graphotherapy the person must have to leave proper space between two words this must not be less than 0.5 cm.

Fig. 6.1.B.i.

(ii)   Such person does not have proper mental ability of creativity using contemporarily forming point of views and opportunities provided by current situations. Since lacking such views, the artistic nature of the person is not observed in active form. The trait revealed by handwriting as handwriting is not observed in manic form at any place. These people do not have any interest in art, music, literature, writing etc. Therefore, it is great need to improve interest in any one of them or in all of them. There is following doodle as graphotherapy –

Fig. 6.1.B.ii.

These are slightly rightward slanted curved lines should be practiced with slow speed initially, and then speed should be increased gradually. The practice pattern is 2-5 minutes 4-6 times a day.

(iii)   There are least factors of happiness available to such person and around as well. Happiness plays important role in overcoming the emotional stress and in maintaining proper blood circulation to the brain as well. Such person pays quite more intimation on their contemporary target or objectives occur until emotional stress and these people also have high curiously about coming condition due to which they become much emotionally stressed along. This is depicted by handwriting as presence of many sudden breaks in handwriting sample. It is needed to make person happy by creating new trait. The mode of perception must not be serious.

There is following doodle to create the trait of happiness as graphotherapy –

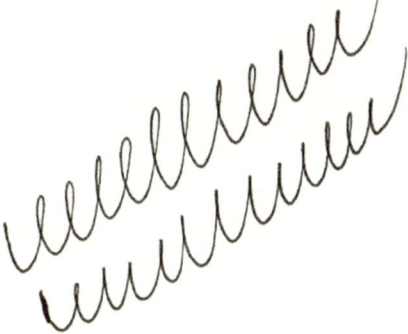

Fig. 6.1.B. iii

This is upward going on 30^0-45^0. The elevation should not be less than .5 cm and should be practiced with high speed 2-5 times and 4-6 times a day.

(iv)   Internally such people are more reactive that hardly come out in spite of being more expressive. Through trait of expressiveness, their real emotions could not be expressed completely in easy way. That is why the incomplete form of negativity stimulates the heart and circulation. Incomplete expression of emotions becomes so serious because of emotional stress changes its forms to be completely expressed or not according to the conditional demand. These changed forms of expressiveness either positive or negative are very cause of emotional stress. The trait revealed in handwriting as some letters of handwriting show abnormally big outgrowth not in regular fashion with abnormal vibration in handwriting due to expectation of coming unwanted situations and conditions.

This is necessary normalize the reactive conditions. To do it there is following doodle as a graphotherapy –

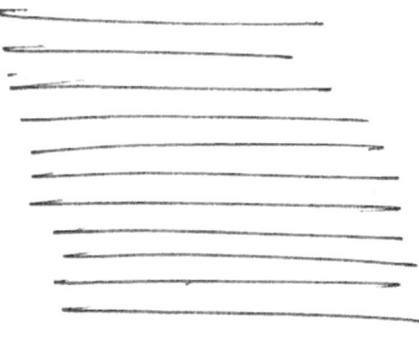

Fig. 6.1.B.iv

These are simple straight lines, which should draw with slow speed for 2-5 minutes 4-6 times a day. During practice there is fact which should be kept in mind that the space among lines would be homogeneous.

C ANGINAL SYNDROME

In this disorder sudden sever pain arises in chest, sometimes it has physical cardiac cause but it's nature is psychophysiological and it get started on this form. Gradually it shifts from psychophysiological to physical ground and many physical factors become observed causing this. As on psychophysiological level there would be many types of emotional conflicts behind major emotional causes of this disorder. Apart from these conflicts there would be other causes like weak immune system of body that fully depends on emotional system of body, irregularities in social conditioning processes conducted by person and proper and definite feelings of symbolic self-expression in every condition any conflict.

CHAPTER - 3

Essential hypertension

This is very common psychophysiological disorder. Without clear physical cause, hypertension is called Essential Hypertension. In this disorder blood pressure becomes increased and then person complaints of headache, irritation, depression, suffocation etc. There are many psychological causes of essential hypertension that is categorized in psychosomatic disorder as its base is completely psycho.

There are many theories to define this disorder. According to Innes (1969) some people keep storm of anger and rage in their inside although from the outside also as they are very calm. Such person has high possibilities of getting into the clutch of hypertension. The study says that they have close relation with their mother, dependent on, lack of confidence and show perfectionist behavior habit in order to computation of lack of confidence and insecurity. To save themselves from difficulties of life they consume drug with being consumer of food glut means it can said they may have addiction of eating.

Symptoms revealed in handwriting – Generally, the person of hypertension shows the upward going signature because of having high ambition but alignment of words has fluctuation because of being no proper correlation between their high ambitions and running conditions of circumstances, the phenomenon results intermittent irritation occurred for long duration to the person. Due to having clear and high ambition the person is highly allocated towards their goal and keeps himself in hurry which result spacing among words and another controversy observed that is occurrence of laid 'c' due to having strong sociality by nature in handwriting with signature segmentation. In order to this, their signature should be in two segments but seen not like that i.e. single segmented. However, they have strong logic power as shown by isolated letter but there is lack of uphill slants.

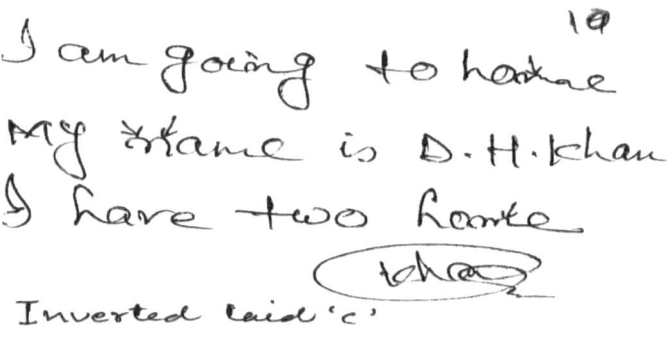

Fig. 6.2

GRAPHOTHERAPIES - There is following sets o graphotherapies –

(i)   Because of being not proper correlation between their high ambitions and running conditions, the person has least possibilities of being succeeded. On being unsuccessful in achieving particular goal of life or target results him lack of confidence, insecurity and to compensate that the persons show perfectionist behavior. Therefore, there is need of proper correlation between their high ambition and running condition. There is following doodle as graphotherapy –

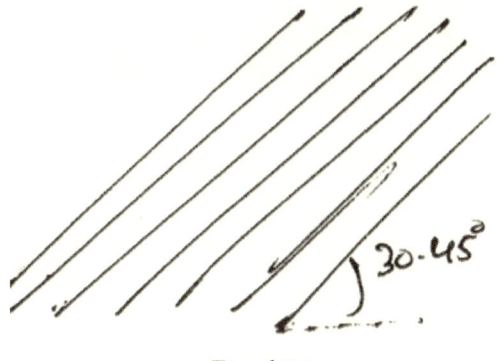

Fig. 6.2.i

There are right slanted lines between 30⁰- 45⁰, which should be practiced with normal speed for 2-5 minutes 4-6 times a day.

(ii)　Normally such person has low enthusiasm depicted by at randomly placed t-bar but not seen more than half. Enthusiasm plays important role in keeping person in form of proud in positive way to launch for better goal or achieving some marvelous things.

There is following doodle as graphotherapy –

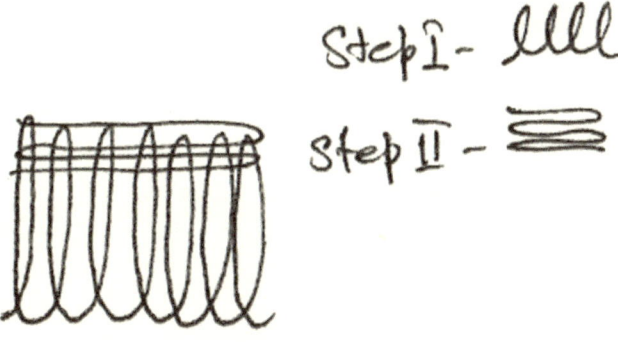

Fig. 6.2.ii

The second step doodle must be upward going. Whole doodle must be practiced with slow speed for 2-5 minutes 4-6 times a day.

(iii) Condition born mental overlapping is also a serious problem for person with hypertension. Due to lack of mental resting phase, mind feels quite more problem for preparing layout for next coming condition or situation. Such person keeps himself always in hurry. The space among words is observed less than 0.5 cm.

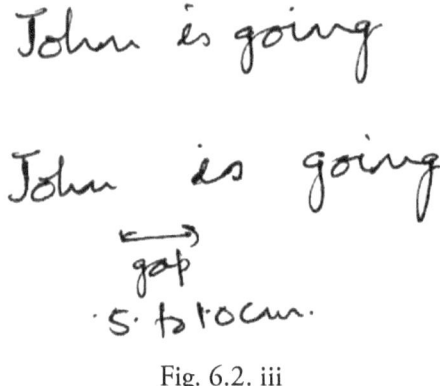

Fig. 6.2. iii

As a graphotherapy the person has to mind the spacing which must to be less than .5 cm among words.

(iv) Sociality of such person has controversial form. By nature, they are social where as in behavior this is not seen in active form. The trait revealed in handwriting there are many laid 'c' in handwriting where as signature is in single segmented.

Therefore, as a graphotherapy they should have to sign their signature in two segments in simple form. That must not be stylish especially that must not be encircled.

Fig. 6.2.iv

The person who has encircled signature may have problem of hypertension, which may lead high possibility of kidney failure, brain hemorrhage, paralysis and so on.

Chapter – 4

Psychophysiologocal Endocrine Disorder

There is direct correlation between state of mind (status of mood, anxiety, confusion etc.) and biochemistry of body. Status of biochemistry is directly determined by endocrine system and responsible for every change either positive or negative and whatever of other types occurred. Endocrine status directly depends upon the emotions determined by circumstances. Behavior of person also directly affects endocrine status. Mode of action and reaction are directly determined by endocrine status.

Endocrine disorder stricken individuals often feel fluctuation in their 'state of mind' regarding any or many concerns. It seems like because of just biochemical imbalance as it is commonly explained. However, all fluctuations occur just because of external stimuli rather than internal. The occurring fluctuations in state of mind within the individual are owing to alteration on perception format, which is strongly in the process of emotional mechanism of individual since initial stages leads to fluctuation in state of mind depicted clearly by handwriting.

It is commonly supposed that many individuals suffering from endocrine problems may also have psychiatric issues as they complaint and show its symptoms like mood, anxiety and other disorders. However, handwriting does not depict symptoms of psychiatric issues because different and specific symptoms of endocrine disorders are deciphered by handwriting due to reflex action. On this basis, it can be said that feeling of psychiatric problems are just false and on curing endocrine problems psychiatric issues go away automatically. Due to dependency of endocrine status on state of mind, it may be apparently visible but not such serious to get individual under intense psychiatric medication and on curing endocrine problems, psychiatric issues disappear automatically.

If endocrine system affects our emotional system, likewise very this way the endocrine system can be affected by emotional system. On bringing change in emotional system through Emotional Engineering understanding emotional mechanism of unique personality, the endocrine disorders are curable.

The endocrine disorder are classified in this category especially disorders in secretion of hormones may be either in hyper or hypo.

Symptoms shown in Handwriting - The person with hormonal disorder especially hyper secretion show following designating features in handwriting –

Fig. 6.3

a. Either person has tinny or very big handwriting which reveals the self-centeredness and over external factor centeredness respectively. They pay either quite enough more intention on themselves or on most of the external factors.

b. Homogenous rhythm is observed in handwriting, which is maintained carefully. In fact such people are very punctual towards their duties whatever they are treated obey and keep continue their punctuality accordingly. They deliver their duty on fixed time but they much difficulty in accepting to bring any change in their routine. Their body is completely conditioned with the time.

c. Due to being self-centeredness and paying quiet more intention on their duties, condition born mental overlapping resulted. However, this is not prominent in unknown circumstances, which are revealed by foreign tongue (English) script that has different format of handwriting rather than mother language (Hindi).

d. They have signature very little and slight upward going, the fact reveled by that their ambition carefully correlated with their routine functions. This is significant property of tinny handwriting while in context of bigger handwriting people are more focused on visible conditional factors instead of being on ambition. That results blurred ambition.

Psycolysiological Endocrine Disorder – Tinny Handwriting/ Very Big Handwriting + Homogenous rhythm of handwriting + Lesser Spacing (hindi) + Little Signature/ Bigger Signature.

GRAPHOTHERAPIES - There are following doodles as graphotherapies to reform its psychological causes –

(i) Generally the handwriting of such person is observed very tinny due to being highly self-centered. They are highly selective about conditional factors regarding themselves. They do high efforts towards being conditioned according to situational demand. The speed of handwriting is also observed less than normal due to more paying intention on those conditions related to them along. Both type of conditional status must be broken. There is following doodle as graphotherapy to reform this trait –

Fig. 6.3.i

These are not same lines in length, which should be practiced with high speed. The length of lines should be between 2 to 5 cm. the pattern should of practice should be 2-5 minutes 4-6 times a day.

(ii) Slight manic form of handwriting is observed in such people, which reveal high efforts unskilled form of artistry with having least attraction. The artistry hardly correlates with the nature of person. This necessary to make it natural and according to that form. The artistry of person must not be time bounded and under high punctuality. It must be natural and in attractive form.

Therefore, person is needed to form the natural artistic form that he could be independent and break the hard time bound adapted routine. There is following doodle as a graphotherapy –

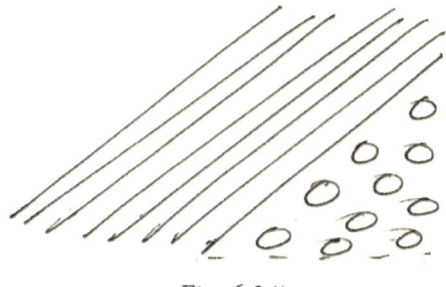

Fig. 6.3.ii

These are slanted lines and then circles. These should be practiced with high speed for 2-5 minutes 4-6 times a day.

(iii) There is low enthusiasm observed in handwriting as shown in lower t-bar in "t" at half or less than half. The fact reveals the due to strong punctuality, the persons do not have proper carefulness about their enthusiastic personal specification which results consideration of all factors which would be concerning with them by any mean. As the persons having situation completed strong punctuality, the form of situation or condition still being unidentified regarding specified enthusiastic presentation on different matters. Therefore, enthusiasm must be always high. As a graphotherapy the person must place t-bar more than half during writing.

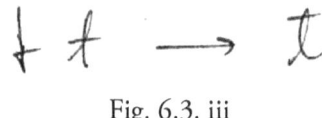

Fig. 6.3. iii

Such people do not establish themselves properly in different situations, which are reflected in handwriting as non-underlined signature and homogeneous rhythm. In fact respite of self-establishment they adopt themselves according to situational demand. So there is very feeble possibility of getting the situation changed according to the person, in reverse of this the people change themselves accordingly and go to compromise with situations easily.

(iv) To reform this trait, the person must sign their signature underline as well as they must also try to keep high speed of signature as much as they can.

Fig. 6.3.iv

CHAPTER – 5

Mild Dehydration

Mild dehydration is a condition of body in which the amount of water becomes less than its adequate amount. By the way immediately it would not damage more but in long term its affects become visible in result of many physical disorders. However, in some cases it has behavioral and emotional causes like irritation, violation, anxiety and irrelevant expectations from the related persons. Mild dehydration is comparatively more occurs in female than male. Because of social and behavioral reasons, females think on getting more water, there would be more possibilities to make water, which would be quite difficulty while she will be outside home and due to being more careful towards her all concerns and related ones having some strong expectations along. After certain limit its effects become started visible in body.

Mild dehydration may cause following problems -

a. High possibilities of stone formation in gale-bladder or in kidney due to high concentration
b. Chronic constipation
c. High irritation due to more sensitivity
d. High possibility of cancer formation the body
e. Problem in disposal of toxins yielded by many biochemical reactions
f. Problem of disposal of distorted hormones.
g. Heart problem due to increased blood viscosity

h. More muscular pain due to improper ca-circulation among actin and myosin

i. High viscous blood and hypertension

j. High possibilities of joint problem, etc.

SYMPTOM REAVELED BY HANDWRITING - There of following significant features revealed by handwriting-

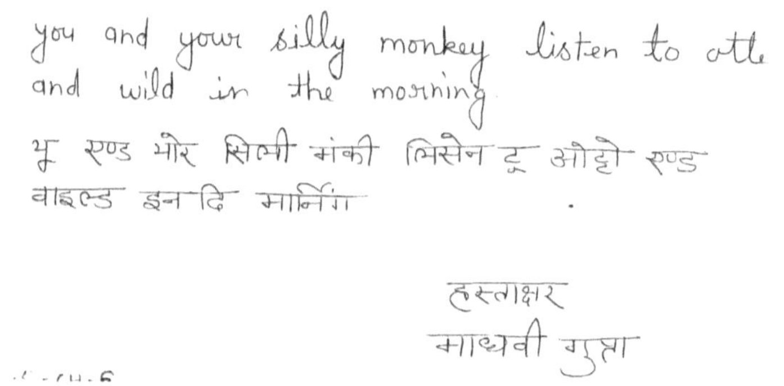

Fig. 6.4

(i) There are enough more conditional and situational factors under consideration of such people. They do not have ability to sort them out according to their own self. There are high possibilities of considering many of unpleasant subjects, which must have to be sorted out either subconsciously or consciously. Such activities are quite abnormal because it causes high intention of finding out answers of all questions which are reflected in handwriting as slight vibration and blunt ending in many letters like in d, n, t, and a.

Such people have strong logic power and want to justify everything according to own self. The trait depicted by handwriting as isolated letter in many words. There are many unjustified facts and unanswered questions remain left even on using strong reasonable efforts cause violation, irritation and anger. The phenomenon result extra sweating and loss of water from body.

(ii)   The person with problem of mild dehydration has improper responsibility feeling means they look for either substitute of their responsibilities or way to be escaped from. They get their responsibilities in bigger shape paying more importance. The trait revealed in handwriting as many isolated letter observed in the many words. Many blunt endings are observed just after isolation with acute folds. As the phenomenon recalls facts just on proper logical ground, person becomes violent and obstinate towards making situation in favor of him or herself along.

(iii)   Most significant feature of mild dehydration is slow speed of handwriting depicts paying extra intention on every topic and factors having specific point of view. It is quite difficult for such person to over look many unwanted factors and events. As they should have to leave many of them, they consider all of them with extra intention having anxiety, irritation, fear, violation or stress. Such abnormalities cause more sweating, making water and hormonal imbalance.

Mild dehydration - Wider Letters + Isolated Letters + Incomplete Loop in 's' + Slow Speed of Writing

GRAPHOTHERAPIES - There is following graphotherapies –

(I)   Such person has condition born confidence, which is reveled in handwriting as slow speed of writing and isolated letters in many words. The facts are recalled on strongly hard efforts of person towards finding out the some favorable logic or define events according to themselves. To strong their confidence, the strong confidence should be part of their basic instinct.

There is following doodle as a graphotherapy to do it –

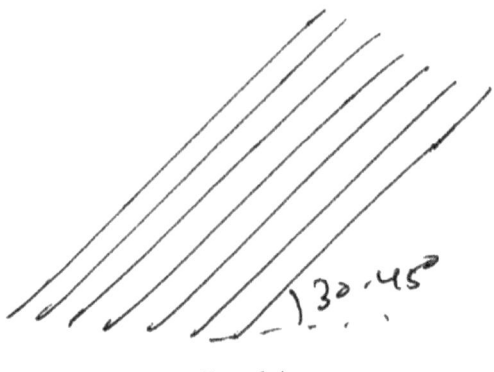

Fig. 6.4.i

These are slanted lines on 30^0- 45^0, which should be practiced with high speed with having fact in mind the homogeneous spacing among two lines for 2-5 minutes 4-6 times a day.

(II)   Such people are hard expressive. They could not express themselves completely due to getting not favorable situation or unsuitability as they expect. Such unexpressed emotions react internally in psychosomatic form or may go to create mood disturbance, anxiety and stress. All these abnormalities become cause of hypertension. The trait revealed in handwriting as most of letters are completely closed and looking as high intention paid to make closed strictly except on letter that is 'o'.

To minimize anxiety, stress and hypertension expressiveness is very necessary for such people. There is following graphotherapy to make them expressive –

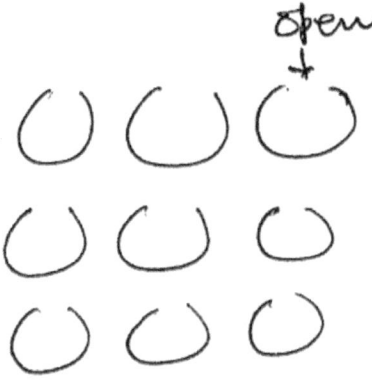

Fig. 6.4.ii

These are open circles from upper side. It should be practiced with slow speed for 2-5 minutes 4-6 times a day. Circle should be made bigger.

(III)   There are many unpleasant events in memory of such person and around them as well. Those are often recalled time to time by the person or compel to recall for analyzing again and again to define or redefine all of them according to themselves. The process is repeated to find out such factor by which they could satisfy their ego. It directly means all these processes are directly controlled by ego factor. The status of trait is depicted by quite bigger backstroke, speed of handwriting quite lesser than normal and if there is no dotted mark is observed in signature.

The person should have to be free from such unpleasant memories. To make them there is following doodle as a graphotherapy –

Fig. 6.4. iii

These are flag like doodle having forwarded its corona. It is slight left slanted. These should be practiced with normal speed 2-5 times 4-6 times a day.

(IV) Such people have negative attitude towards their most of own circumstances and next too. Due to which they become frustrated and pessimist. The trait revealed by handwriting as quite bigger loop, made by relevant letters like 'g' & 'y'. The homogeneousness is observed as in disturbed format in handwriting. Whereas signature may be observed in many segmented and in straight line. Because of negative impact of several isolated negative factors on basic assessments of such people.

Therefore, to create the appropriate attitude rather than positive attitude as a graphotherapy they do never make big loop in g y and z and tail of letter must cross the head of letter "g".

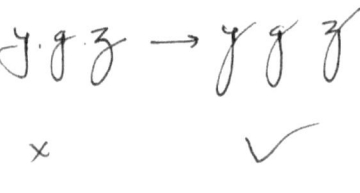

Fig. 6.4 iv

(V) Such people always escape from their responsibility and in spite of having strong compulsion to meet them out. The trait is revealed incomplete loop in 's' which is observed as intended to make them complete but those could not be due to improper feeling of self utility about objectives which would be condition or person born, words are made bigger because of considering many conditional factors regarding their use and handwriting is not in manic form.

To make them responsible there is following doodle as graphotherapy-

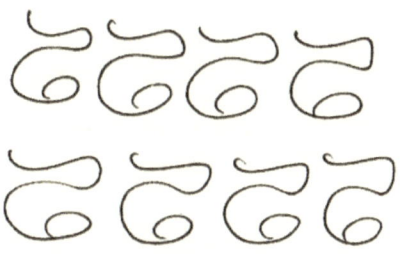

Fig. 6.4 v

This is the single unit of doodle and should be practiced with slow speed. The practice pattern is 2-5 minutes 4-6 time a day.

(VI) In such people suffering from mild dehydration thought fullness is not observed in homogenous form. Huge fluctuations are seen in this trait. The 'l', 'd' and 'k'. People who has loop in these letters have strong thoughtfulness. No homogeneousness observed through such letters loops are not formed in regular fashion. Due to not being non homogeneous thoughtfulness person has quite more difficulties in being happy and after all happiness is very necessary as great emotional tool to run properly traits of non-violence and keeping logic power in rhythmic form. There is following doodle as a graphotherapy –

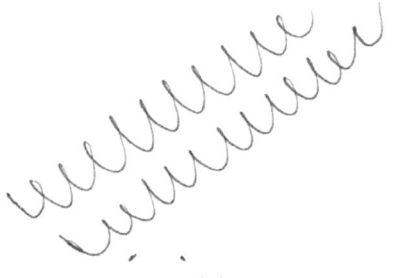

Fig. 6.4.vi

The shape of loop must keep in mind, which would be between 1- 5 to 2 cm. formation of loop, is must not be missing. Doodle must be upward going on slant of 30-45⁰, should be practiced for 2-5 minutes 4-6 times a day. Speed of doodle should be normal.

(VII) With the graphotherapies such people also signs their signature shortly i.e. initial forms for better expressiveness and hastened concluding their campaigns. Signature must be upward going, underlined and under marked.

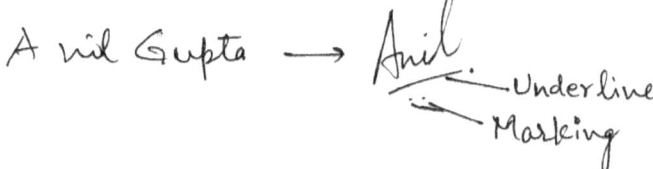

Fig. 6.4.vii

ANNEXURE

I would like to discuss two examples of very complicated cases were chronic and under deep psychiatric medication. However, there are so many cured cases of different categories including all types but cases about which I am going to discussing here as example are the most the complicated and even cured just by Emotional Engineering within few months. One is psychologically very complicated having multiple disorders and other one had complication psycho and psychosomatic both. The word complication was being used by psychiatrist during treatment. Therefore, patient was bound to consume medicines. However, for "Emotional Engineering" there is no meaning of complication. It is very easy to cure any complicated disorder like other by "Emotional Engineering" with full of mental empowerment.

Case - 1

Name of Client	-	R.P. G.
Address	-	XXXXXXXXXXXXXXXXXX
Age	-	33 Years
Qualification	-	M.A., B.Ed
Occupation	-	Teaching
Marital Status	-	Married
Gander	-	Male
Diagnosis	-	Panic Disorder, Episodic Mood status including 7 forms, Absurd Talking, Violent since 4 years.

Case History

Psychologically this case was very complicated. Client was suffering from "multiple mental disorders" and under deep psychiatric medication since last 4 years.

Clint is very simple man and ordinarily highly educated. About 4 years back he was going to 300 Km long to appear in competitive exam by bus to get job. Reaching near around 100 Km. long suddenly he jumped off the running bus and got injured. People around him got him in hospital then on coming him back conscious, he made reach to his home city. Here then he was diagnosed as having psychiatric problem then got admitted to mental hospital. After 15 days he was released but psychiatric medication was still continue until my consultation.

you and your silly monkey listen to otte and wild in the morning

Therapeutic Graphological Research Report to read twice a day

1. Time to time you should change your circumstances as much as you can, using conditional factors in which you live and work. The change may be of any type. You have to know only reason behind it. Because the confidence of person is highly depending upon conditions and circumstances, which have negative impacts. The trait is depicted by handwriting as –

   (i) The English sample has straight alignment where as Hindi is downward going.
   (ii) Gap between two words are more in English than Hindi.

(iii) English signature is in straight line where as Hindi signature is in upward going.

(iv) Forms of letters are more same in Hindi than English.

(v) Many deformations are observed in both Hindi and English samples.

2. Make strong your ego. Some decision should be taken just on ego on which no compromise should be occurred and at the same time do not underestimate yourself. The ego of person is not in healthy form as it should be. The handwriting depicts this trait as –

(i) First letter is quiet bigger than rest of others.

(ii) Speed of handwriting is less than normal.

(iii) Area covered by signature more than normal in length.

3. Do not try to get instant solution of any problem. Problem should be studied properly and on not getting solutions on this be inactive for some times, solution will start to come automatically. Because person has weak trait of solution seeking with high activeness is depicted in handwriting as –

(i) No specific deformation observed in handwriting.

(ii) More than normal area covered by signature.

(iii) Signature is in more than two segments.

(iv) Needle 'n', 'm' humps observed in handwriting.

4. Live in present and do not compare your present with your past. Use available resources in new way and by new methods. Because person seems better past he has than present that results strong affection with past in person. It is revealed in handwriting as –

(i) There are two types of letters in handwriting and some letters of signature are tried to decorate unnecessary.

(ii) Speed of handwriting slow.

(iii) More wide letters in handwriting sample.

(iv) Smaller shape of letters.

5. Imagine pleasure about coming conditions and try to find out point of pleasures by strong efforts. Because person wants to look for pleasure but he feels danger because of weak traits pleasure he has. The trait is depicted in handwriting as –

   (i)   Slight rhythmic flow in handwriting.
   (ii) More gap among two successive words in handwriting sample.
   (iii) Some letters has upstrokes covers whole letter.

6. Avoid using anything for long time and ensure changes what you use after certain time. Because person uses many things for long time with least duration, therefore impact of persistency is prominently observed. The trait is depicted in handwriting as –

   (i)   Letters of handwriting are not elongated and erected.
   (ii) Hindi signature in upward going.
   (iii) Slow speed of handwriting.
   (iv) No positive deformation is observed in handwriting.

7. Respect your own wills and ensure their expressions. Because person has obstructions in expressions without self improvement. The trait is revealed in handwriting as –

   (i)   No shield in handwriting whereas English signature has.
   (ii) The English signature has outgrowths.

8. Discuss any or many matters with someone else. You may select person according to your convenience. Because no proper rational exchange is observed in person that results process of coming new ideas is not in active form. Handwriting depicts this trait as –

   (i)   Only two or three letters of middle part of signature are compressed.
   (ii) Letters are not elevated properly.

9. Do not compromise with unwanted conditions as much as you can. If there is compulsion to you regarding this concern, make it reasonable and time bounded. On finishing its committed time, end your compromise and start work on options. Because person is not clear on his compromises and has confused mind on his matters of priorities. This is depicted in handwriting as –

   (i)   Signature is not underlined.
   (ii) Upper zone of handwriting has needle extension.
   (iii) Handwriting has both acute and circular folds abnormally.
   (iv) Uphill slants are not in proper number.

10. Keep gap of 10 to 15 minutes between successive conditions in both acquainted and non-acquainted conditions. Because there are contradictory impact of both acquainted and non-acquainted conditions on the person. This is revealed in handwriting as –

    (i)   Gap between two successive words are abnormal i.e. more in English sample where as lesser in Hindi sample.

11. Campaigns you run ensure definite conclusion of that because person does not conclude his campaigns properly. Most of them are left in midterm which is depicted by handwriting as –

    (i)   Words are not completed in same fashion.

12. Strictly and openly follow the social decorum like saying thanks, sorry etc. because person is not properly humble. The trait is depicted by handwriting as –

    (i)   There are abnormal acute folds in handwriting sample.
    (ii) Letters are closed.
    (iii) No specific deformation is observed in handwriting sample.

13. Change your thoughts according to time demand because person has condition born obstinacy, revealed by handwriting as –

    (i)   Handwriting is going upwards first and then bends slightly.
    (ii)   Some letters are in hanging position.
    (iii)   First letter of signature is quiet bigger than rest of others.
    (iv)   Letters are slightly stretched.

14. Keep yourself away from loneliness because person is self centered and condition born obstinacy while he also like this which is depicted by handwriting as –

    (i)   Long down stroke in first letter.
    (ii)   No prominent upstroke in upper zone.
    (iii)   No s-loop in appropriate shape.

15. Share your responsibilities because person has self focused responsibilities and complexes of relevant bases, revealed in handwriting as –

    (i)   Small s-loop is observed.
    (ii)   In signature only first letter is bigger rather than other relevant letters.
    (iii)   Loop is connected with other letters and words.

16. Read kid's literatures (like kid's stories, poems and enjoy them) because person does not has extension system of his studiousness depicted by handwriting as –

    (i)   Signature and handwriting both are determined by baseline.
    (ii)   Speed is controlled by rhythm of handwriting.
    (iii)   Signature is not downward going.

Graphotherapies – Following Graphotherapies are given to practice 4 to 6 times a day just for 2 – 4 minutes each.

(i)

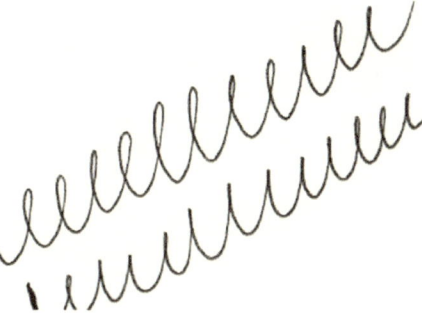

¼ii½

¼iii½

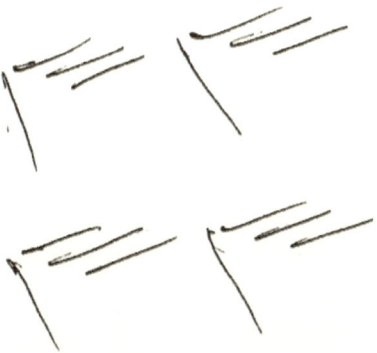

¼iv½

¼v½

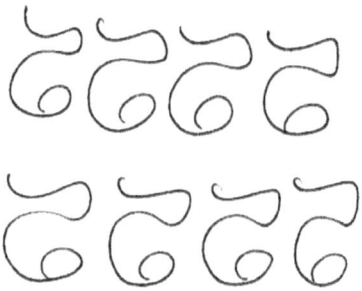

¼vi½

(vii)

Result – On following instructions given in the report and practicing graphotherapies. Just after 15 days -

(i)   The dose of psychiatric became just half.

(ii)   He started his home tuition job which was stopped since getting hospitalized.

(iii)   After next 15 days he was kept on just one drug.

(iv)   About next 15 days he was completely free from medication.

(v)   He resumed his private teaching job again.

(vi)   Now he is completely normal and has no need of medication.

Case – 2

Name of Client	-	A.K.M.
Age	-	30 Years
Address	-	XXXXXXXXXXXXXXXX
Qualification	-	B.A. II
Date	-	12 April 2012
Occupation	-	Private Teaching
Marital Status	-	Married
Diagnosis / Complaint	-	Depression based on Obsession and Eosinophil count around 13% since 13 years

Case History

This was also very complicated and intricate case of psycho and psychosomatic disorders. Because of anxiety and mood disorder, gastric problem aroused and after sometimes his immune system was suppressed that resulted high count of eosinophil took place and that was persisted by around 20% for about one decade.

In 1999 client went to Mumbai to earn money. Regarding that concern he started learning tailoring. After some days, he felt problem in his stomach and consulted physician then started medication. On getting no benefit until 3 months he back to his village home and started medication under other physician. In mean time, he felt some additional problems in eating some dishes like curd, rice, onion, reddish that problem in breathing, heavy sneezing, coughing etc. Then he was advised to go for TLC-DLC test of blood. In report, his Eosnophilia count was 11%. He kept continue his gastric treatment. About year later, on getting no benefit of gastric treatment, he was told by physician may have problem of depression because in depression gastric problem is common phenomenon. Then he come to take psychiatric treatment and consulted psychiatrist. In mean time, he again got his blood test and found his eosnophilia count was increased by 13%. This count was remaining persistent for 13 years. After eating curd, rice, onion, reddish etc he had to take a dose of "betnesol" to get relief. His psychiatric medication was still continued but after few years on getting no benefit he changed psychiatrist. Even after few years later he had to again change psychiatrist on no benefits and this changing event was repeated after next few years, instead of benefit case was becoming even more and more serious gradually. Ultimately, after 13 years on getting defeated with deep psychiatric and gastric medication, he consulted me and just within 2 months, he was completely cured.

Handwriting sample -

You and your silly monkey listen to atta and wild in the morning. Go for the best.

Anil Kumar Maurya

First Blood report

श्याम पैथालोजी   Date 9-3-1999

Pt. Name ....Mr. Manish Kumar......

Age ......14yrs............ Sex..M............

Ref by Dr ....Gupta.........

Specimen.....Blood & R.E. Test.........

Haematological Report

	Normal Values in Adults
T.L.C. 9,400 Per cu m.m.	4-11, OCO cu m m
Differential leukocyte count	
Polymorphs .. 44 ... %	P = 40-60 %
Lymphocytes .. 20 ... %	L = 20-40 %
Eosinophils... 44 ... %	E = 2 - 6 %
Monocytes .. 00 ... %	M = 0 - 2 %

Second Blood Report

HAEMOGLOBIN		12.3 Gm%	[11.5-18 Gm%]
TOTAL LEUKOCYTE COUNT		8600 /Cumm	[4000-11000 /Cumm]
DIFF. LEUKOCYTE COUNT			
NEUTROPHILS		59 %	[40-75 %]
LYMPHOCYTES		20 %	[20-45 %]
MONOCYTES	(L)	01 %	[2-10 %]
EOSINOPHILS	(H)	20 %	[1-6 %]
BASOPHILS		00 %	
E.S.R. (IN ONE HOUR)	(H)	18 mm	[2-11 mm]

Third Blood Report –

Haemoglobin	13.5 Gm%	(12 - 18 Gm%)
Total Leukocyte Count	7200 /Cumm	(4000 - 11000 /Cumm)
Diff. Leukocyte Count		
Neutrophils	80 %	[40 - 75 %]
Lymphocytes	26 %	[20 - 45 %]
Monocytes	01 %	[1 - 10 %]
Eosinophils	13 %	[1 - 6 %]
Basophils	00 %	(0 - 1 %)

First Psychiatrist

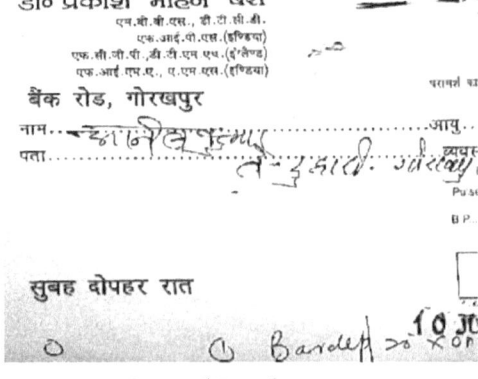

Second Psychiatrist

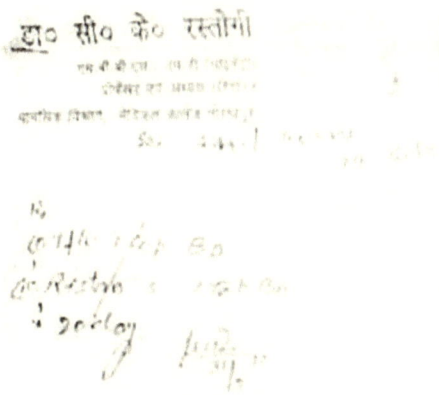

Gastric Physician

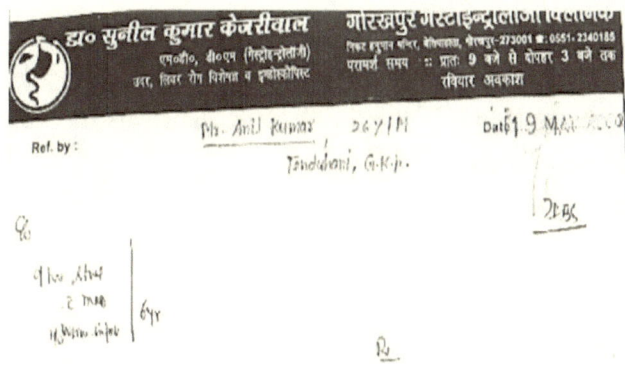

Given Therapeutic Graphological Personality Research Report to read Twice a Day

1. **Confidence** – Your confidence completely depends on conditions. Therefore, on being slight change in conditions, your confidence becomes affected if change is positive then confidence becomes positively changed if negative then negative. So, keep conditions under your full control. Mind it; all things must be according to you. As far as possible ensure changes as you want and regarding this concern you need not to consult any one.

2. **Reasonability and Conditions** – Logically keep your and related conditions always in simplest situation. Pay attention that no situation is like that either that could not be understandable or make other understandable.

3. **Communication** – You have great need to communicate other general people. So, use most of general conditional factors in that. Theme of communication can be anything. The gradual increment in number of communication people is necessary for you.

4. **Straightforwardness** – Use this trait as more as you can. On every subject there must be your clear point of view. Don't hide any matter from your wife also.

5. **Ambition** – Strong and clear ambition about self that after certain time in what form would you like to see you. This must be absolutely clear and it may be of any field. There is no difference that either you are capable for that or not.

6. **Trait of Proud** – There must be number of reasons of proud of family's background, economic status, education, social status or may be anything. If you don't have then you should create own causes of proud on self.

7. **Pleasure** – Find out the points of pleasure in all of conditions. It is not necessary that if most of people enjoy any condition that will also be your point of pleasure. There must your own criteria and form of point of pleasure according to you. Imagine pleasure and find out point pleasure about coming conditions.

8. **Obstinacy** - Give proper shape your obstinacy and this should be absolutely correlated with your ambition and logic power. At the same time, it should not be reflected in your general behavior but use this maximum for ambition and subject.

9. **Use of Things** – Use any thing for certain time and limit and after that limit of satisfaction there must be definitely change. Same fact should be applied among the closed people. You can determine this change according to your economic status.

10. **Plans** – Instead of making many plans at a time, make only one plan at a time and work according to that.

11. **Interval** – Keep Interval of 10 to 15 minutes between two successive conditions. Not less than 10 minutes and not more than 15 minutes.

12. **Task and Goal Setting** – Divide your task into small parts and make it time bounded goals that could be accomplished in the time limit and within the limit meet your goal out.

13. **Self-Specialty** – You must know about your specialty with their limitations also and if you are in those conditions with supposing yourself competent then your presentation will be best.

14. **Rational Assistance** – You cannot get rational assistance from every one through communication. Regarding this context you should have to get of experts and close to you. The number of such people in your circle should be around 5 to 8.

15. **Trait of Compromising** – Your behavior and presentation should be like such that you need not compromise and if this is compulsory for then go for time bound compromise. Time finished compromise finish.

16. **Exploration** – Firstly you have to get skill in particular field then after consistency find out the field in which you can give your best performance. Always pay attention that this is far-reaching strategy.

17. **Doubt** – It is very necessary of doubt in small amounts. But you should not have to react on those until getting proof.

18. **Loneliness** – As far as possible avoid loneliness. If it is necessary for you then have all instruments of communication.

19. **Trait of self imposition on others** – Avoid imposing self on other on any matter. Thought this trait is weak in you nevertheless don't compel others either on any matter or regarding self.

20. **Thoughts** – On coming new thoughts on any matter in your mind, right down all anywhere or in a diary and read those all time to time.

21. **Sociality** – Do not miss opportunity of meeting any one, definitely meet them and talk to them with full of pleasure.

Given Graphotherapies – To Practice 4 to 6 times a day following graphotherapies have been given just for 2 to 4 minutes each.

(i)

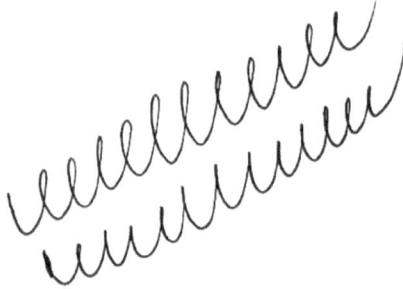

¼ii½

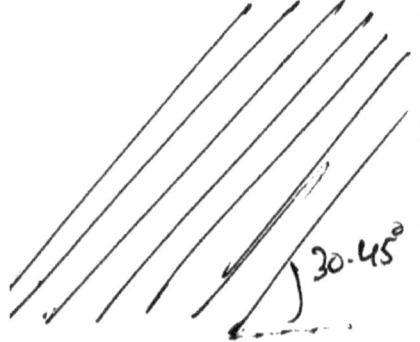

¼iii½

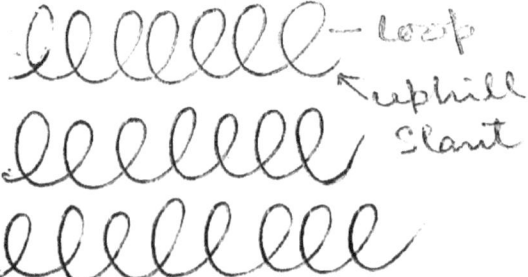

¼iv½

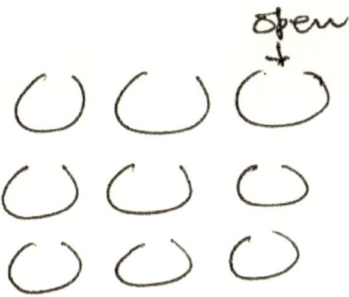

¼v½

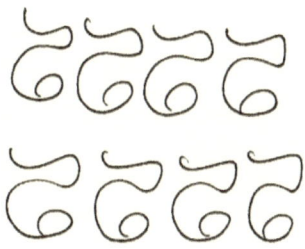

¼vi½

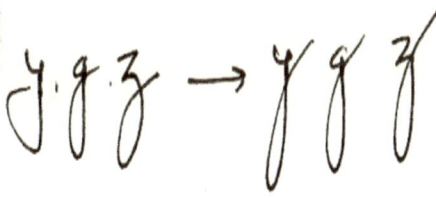

(vii)

(viii)

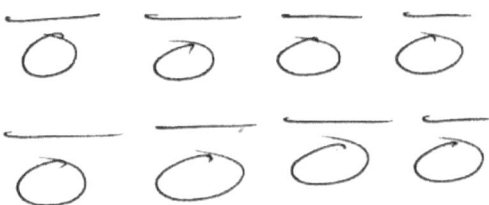

(ix)

(x)

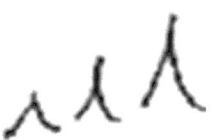

Result - Just after two months client got following changes –
Blood report of two month later after treatment of "Emotional Engineering"

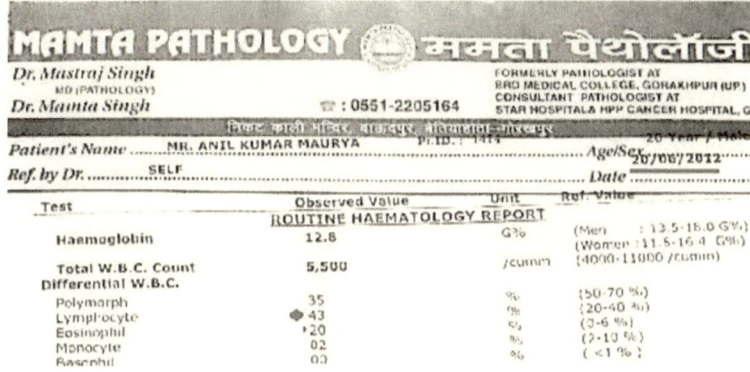

(i) He became completely rid of psychiatric problems which resulted end of all types of medication psychiatric and gastric as well. Need of any drug was no more to him.

(ii) Firstly his Lymphocyte count in blood increased by 100% became 43% first time and later on his eosinophil became normal. And he has no problem in taking any dish especially by which he had problem.

(iii) He is living normal life like other healthy person.

INDEX

www.ingramcontent.com/pod-product-compliance
Lightning Source LLC
Chambersburg PA
CBHW030422290526
45786CB00001B/93